Be... ♡ **W9-CGK-756** l 95

Charles Roth

MIND:

the Master Power

Unity Books
Unity Village, Missouri 64065

Unity Books
Unity Village, Missouri 64065

Revised Edition—1984

Cover design by
Jeri Robinson

This book
is gratefully dedicated
to
Elizabeth, my wife.

Contents

Contents

I

Your Untapped Potential

The Bible story of the talents is a familiar one. One servant received five talents, another two, another one. Two of the servants used, or invested, their talents and increased them. The third servant guarded his closely for fear of losing it. Those servants who used and increased their talents were given more, and the servant who fearfully clung to his had it taken away and given to the servant with ten talents.

As many times as you have heard this story, how did you apply it to your own life? If you are like many people, you didn't relate it to your own life at all; perhaps you felt the story referred to people who had some special gift or talent, such as writing or painting or singing.

Yet when Jesus told this parable, He wasn't speaking to a group of artistically talented people.

1

He was speaking to skilled and unskilled workers, farmers, fishermen—ordinary people like you and me—who He knew had *extra*ordinary potentialities within them.

Let us think about five talents or extraordinary potentialities in particular that *you* possess right now. Let us see how you can invest your five talents and double them. And let us explore how you may develop your extraordinary potential to experience the peace of mind, harmony of affairs, and increase in health as well as supply that these talents will earn, that these potentialities will produce.

Talent or extraordinary potential number one: *the talent or ability to think.*

You may say, "What kind of talent is that? Everybody can think; there's no trick to that!" However, that's just the point—*everybody* can think! Remember, Jesus was talking to ordinary people, so the talents He talked about would logically be things that ordinary people possess but may not be using or investing wisely. Besides, there actually is a "trick" to thinking. The "trick" is to think positive thoughts, constructive thoughts, prosperous thoughts, healthy thoughts, and to avoid thinking negative thoughts, destructive thoughts, lack thoughts, sick thoughts!

As an experiment, pretend you are the servant

in Jesus' story. You have been given the talent or ability to think. You can invest this talent wisely and give your attention to thinking constructive thoughts as consistently as you are able, or you can choose to be uninterested in making the effort and just go on as before, remaining just as bad off or as well off as you are today.

If you invest your talent of thinking wisely, you will find that the principle of the parable holds true. The Lord, or law of life, will enhance your life tremendously. If you choose to disregard your talent, that is, not use it wisely, you will probably find that negative thinking dominates your positive thinking, and in the long run things will get worse. In short, that which you have, as Jesus said, will be taken from you. This is not a threat, it is merely the inevitable outworking of law. Increased or accumulated negative thoughts and feelings result in increasingly negative conditions.

2) Talent or potential number two is *the ability to believe.*

It may also seem obvious that everyone has the ability to believe. Again, that is why it is the kind of talent Jesus was talking about—because *everybody* has it!

You must choose what you are going to believe, because belief is the key to your life. You are what you believe. Do you believe yourself to

3

be unhappy, a wallflower, inadequate? Then that is what you are! Are you always "low man on the totem pole"? Are you sickly, weak; do others get the opportunities while life passes you by? Then on your subconscious level of mind, you *believe* that this is the kind of person you are.

You may say, "I don't have to believe it—it's so. Just look at the facts!" But the facts are what they are because of your accepted beliefs.

The time must come—and let it be today— when regardless of the facts, you choose to believe that you are an adequate person, a remarkable person, a successful person, a poised and confident person, because you know that you are a child of God and you choose to believe the teaching of Jesus that God is within you.

What are you going to do with this talent or ability to believe what you choose to believe? Are you just going to bury it, or are you going to use it constructively to believe that God is working through you in everything you do or attempt to do and therefore things will work out in a perfect and successful way? "As you believe, so be it done unto you!"

3. Another talent or extraordinary potential you presently have is *imagination.*

How are you using your imagination? Imagination is called the "scissors of the mind" because,

4

just as you use a pair of scissors on a bolt of material and that material becomes the form that your scissors cut it into, so does your imagination work on the unspecialized substance of God all around you, and that substance becomes to you just the form that your imagination gives it!

Therefore, invest your talent of imagination wisely. See yourself well and strong if presently you are having a health challenge. See yourself making successful sales if you are in business. See yourself poised and confident in some situation that you may be dreading to face.

Again, don't tell yourself that this is childish or unrealistic. We are just beginning to discover the tremendous powers of the mind. Don't be left behind in an age that is limited to what one can see or touch or taste. The new age adds to these the dimensions of mind, and the potentialities of these new dimensions are unlimited.

See yourself as you want to be, and you will become that! *What thou seest, man, become thou must. God if thou seest God; dust if thou seest dust!*

The next talent or untapped potential is *praise and thanksgiving.*

Everyone has the ability to praise things, situations, and people. Let's use this ability well instead of burying it in the land of the unspoken word, the graveyard of good intentions.

Praise and thanksgiving serve to open the connection between you and your good. You see, we are all part of one universal creation. In order to bring good to you, God works through all things, all people, all conditions; and if you are not consciously connected to the divine network, as we might call it, your good cannot easily reach you.

Praise and thanksgiving open the lines; they connect you to the universe of good and thereby to the unrestricted activity of God. Praise your home, your job, your children, your co-workers. Praise your body, praise the efforts of others. Praise God!

To every affirmation of Truth you make, add "I am grateful." To every positive picture you visualize with the talent of your imagination, add "I am grateful." Gratitude is a spiritual enzyme that hastens the fulfillment of your prayer of faith.

The fifth talent or potential is *the ability to pray.*

By prayer, I don't mean just the "Now I lay me down to sleep" kind of prayer. I mean the prayer of quietly going within yourself and realizing your oneness with God. You can do it; anyone and everyone can do it.

Again, let's remember that at the time He gave the parable of the talents, Jesus was talking to all kinds of people—the educated as well as the unlettered, skilled and unskilled, young and old, rich and poor. He knew that each had the untapped potential to dialogue directly with God through prayer.

What a tragedy it is that prayer through the ages has somehow developed into a one-way conversation, with man listing all the people and situations he would like blessed, or sometimes bargaining with God—as if to say, "I will promise to do this or that, if You will take care of this seemingly hopeless situation in a way that gets me off the hook!"

Prayer is more than just talking, except perhaps to "echo" the truths that God has spoken into the depths of your being. These truths may come as affirmations, such as: *There is only one presence and one power, God, the good omnipotent;* or *The light of God guides me into right action in every situation.*

Prayer is experiencing the presence of God in you and as you. Prayer is total surrender to a realization of oneness with God, the creative impulse within the universe.

Of all our talents, prayer is the most dynamic, and yet perhaps the least developed. Take time today and each day to develop and become skilled in your talent to pray. Prayer is so simple; the only difficult thing about it is hurdling the obstacle of procrastination, which can be quite a challenge. But when the desire is great enough, procrastination melts away.

Become still for a moment, and feel yourself as one with all the universe, one with the one Presence, the one Power, the one Life in whom all of us live, move, and have our being. As you do this, you begin to realize the truth, stated over and over again in the Bible, that you are a tremendously wonderful and remarkable person! It is time religion began emphasizing some of the positive aspects of man's nature instead of dwelling on the human faults and frailties that we have yet to overcome.

In Genesis, we read: *Then God said, "Let us make man in our image, after our likeness; and let them have dominion over the fish of the sea, and over the birds of the air, and over the cattle, and over all the earth . . . . " So God created man in his own image, in the image of God he created him . . . .* (Gen. 1:26, 27)

What are we to make of this? Are we to read it and forget it, feeling that it can't possibly be referring to us? I don't think so. I think we ought to ask some questions about the meaning of these words. We need to go within in prayer to the source of all answers.

The above passage from the Bible is saying that

man is made in the image-likeness of God. And if that is true, then you, who are a member of the generic species, man, are made in the image and after the likeness of God. This makes you a very remarkable person, doesn't it? This makes you potentially capable of being successful in anything you undertake.

In Paul's first letter to the Corinthians, he wrote: *Do you not know that you are God's temple and that God's Spirit dwells in you?* (I Cor. 3:16) If the Spirit of God dwells in you, then you certainly are a very remarkable person; you are capable of doing and being much more than you have ever dared dream possible.

Jesus taught that you are a child of God. He said that when you pray, you should begin your prayer with the words, "Our Father." If God is your Father, that makes you God's child, not God's stepchild, but God's very own child and heir.

In fact, Paul used those very words in his letter to the Romans. He wrote: . . . *we are children of God, and if children, then heirs, heirs of God and fellow heirs with Christ* . . . . (Rom. 8:16, 17)

If you have ever prayed the Lord's Prayer and begun it by saying "Our Father," then you are automatically acknowledging that you are a child of God; and being a child of God makes you a very remarkable person. It is logical to assume that you have tremendous potentialities!

But let's go on reacquainting ourselves with the overwhelming evidence in the Bible that you are a remarkable person and that you have as a part of your basic heritage more power and potential mastery over circumstances than you have ever imagined.

Chapter 17, verses 20 and 21, of Luke's Gospel has an important message for us. (Gospel, incidentally, means "good news," and it certainly is good news when we really understand what Jesus was trying to teach us about our spiritual potentialities.)

Being asked by the Pharisees when the kingdom of God was coming, he answered them, "The kingdom of God is not coming with signs to be observed; nor will they say, 'Lo, here it is!' or 'There!' for behold, the kingdom of God is in the midst of you."

I think we cannot be told this tremendous, life-changing, answer-providing truth too often. Doesn't this make you a very remarkable person, if the kingdom of God is, as Jesus said, in the midst of you?

In Paul's letter to the Colossians, he spoke of *Christ in you, the hope of glory.* (Col. 1:27) The

Christ in you that Paul was talking about is the image and likeness of God in you. The Christ in you is the God-self in you. And through the Christ in you, you can do all things.

Would you like to see the Christ in you, the image-likeness of God in you? Although spiritual things cannot be seen, perhaps the following exercise or example will help you to "see" the Christ in you with your mind if not with your physical eyes.

The next time you get a chance, look into a mirror, preferably a full-length mirror. What do you see? Actually, you see many people, or many selves, when you look into a mirror. Sometimes you may see an angry self, sometimes a troubled self, sometimes a determined self. Sometimes, if you are honest, you might see a spoiled child-self with a mixed look of hatred and self-pity.

Yes, there is a sense in which we are many persons—sometimes strong, sometimes weak as jelly. Sometimes we seem filled with boundless faith; other times we seem to demonstrate only the faith of a peanut. No wonder we often get confused and cry out to ourselves: "Who am I? Which one of these persons am I really?"

Let me suggest who you really are. You are that invisible sense of identity, or sense of "I am," or sense of beingness that stands behind all your changing moods and selves. Even though each time you look in the mirror you may see a different you, there is one element that does not change—that changeless element is *you.*

That unchanging sense of identity, of "I Amness," is the Christ in you; it is the central and spiritual core of your being through which you are one with the universal spirit of God, and through which you have access to or are heir to the kingdom of God. The kingdom of God, as Jesus emphatically stated, is *within you.*

We can understand now what Emerson was thinking about when he wrote: *Every man is a divinity in disguise; a god playing the fool.* It is time to stop *playing the fool,* and to start acknowledging, recognizing, and seeking to express the spiritual potential that the Bible so consistently and clearly insists is within you.

You can begin by taking a new look at yourself in your mirror. Face the facts. Accept yourself as you are—but remember that this includes both the self you see in the mirror that may be discouraged or depressed, and the child-of-God "you," the image-and-likeness-of-God "you," the Christ in you.

Remember to look past the facts to the everywhere-present, always active Spirit of God. Look past the changing, changeable you in the mirror to the unchanging Christ in you. Then you can look at whatever in yourself may need changing, or whatever may seem to have you down and discouraged, and say as Paul said: *I can do all things in him who strengthens me.* (Phil. 4:13)

You are a remarkable person indeed, and you possess untapped spiritual potential. You are created in the image-likeness of God, as Genesis states; God's very own Spirit indwells you, as Paul stated; God is your spiritual Parent, as Jesus taught; and you are God's spiritual child.

With all these things going for you, you have the potential for greatness, the potential to be a winner, the potential resources to face and overcome any and every problem or challenge that comes into your life.

As you meditate on your true nature as a spiritual being and a child of God, know for yourself: *I am a very remarkable person, with infinite spiritual potential!*

Through the Looking Glass

How do you see yourself? Young? Old? Underweight? Overweight? Male? Female? The looking glass reflects the outer appearance; but we need not take the appearance to be the ultimate Truth. The Truth is that you are a spiritual being— ageless, deathless, all-conquering!

A looking-glass mind reflects outer conditions, and its thoughts and feelings are shaped to fit them. Thus, through the law of mind action, more painful or limiting conditions are formed.

Starting now, see yourself in a new way. You are greater than the mirror image!

See outer conditions as effects, spent arrows. Let your mind be not a mirror, but a lens through which shines the light of Truth.

Exercise

Relax. Turn your thoughts inward. Say to yourself: *I am going deeper, and deeper, and deeper into the heart of my being.*

In the quietness, visualize your present problem or challenge. Look at the ugly, the painful, the frightening facts; but as you look at them and recognize the tendency to feel the mental pain of fear, regret, or anger, stop and realize that your mind is mirroring only what your eyes perceive. Then turn your head slightly and realize that through the power of thought and feeling, you are actually projecting the image in your looking-glass mind to mold another set of painful, ugly, frightening facts that in turn will be reflected in your mirror mind.

Now think of the quicksilver as being removed from the glass, making your mind no longer a mirror but clear and lucid. Realize now that the Christ in you, the spiritual you, the real you, is looking out through your mind. You see facts and conditions as transient, moldable, ever-changing forms. Just smile at these forms, for the light of Truth streaming through your clear and unclouded mind dissolves the ugliness; fear hurries away as the light is turned on in your thinking. *For now we see in a mirror dimly, but then face to face.* (I Cor. 13:12)

A person's self-image is the way he sees himself. For too long you may have seen yourself as weak, helpless, afraid. As you use these prayer statements, see yourself in the light of Truth.

I see myself in a new way. As a child of God I am guided by His light and wisdom.

I see myself in a new way. As a child of God I am healed by His strength and power.

I see myself in a new way. As a child of God my resources are unlimited.

I see myself in a new way. As a child of God my life is filled with order and happiness.

Benediction Thought

I go forth a new person, no longer bound to the past. Past mistakes and accomplishments are assimilated creatively by the new person that I am.

I go forward into the confronting moment with a

new song of faith in my heart, letting the light of Truth shine through my clear and unclouded mind, and I am grateful!

II

How to Recognize the Christ in You

In the first chapter, we discussed the untapped spiritual potential of the indwelling Christ. I feel led to elaborate on the idea of the Christ within for two reasons: 1) it may be a new idea to many, and 2) even if you are familiar with the idea of the Christ indwelling you, it always helps to think about it from new angles. Somehow this deepens your conviction that indeed there is a directive intelligence *in you* that knows your needs, your abilities, your aspirations, your present limitations; and it is guiding you in the most perfect way possible toward the fulfillment of innate potentialities.

There is a distinction between the man Jesus and the title *Christ*. For example, in Paul's letter to the Colossians, he writes: . . . *the mystery hidden for ages and generations . . . Christ in you, the hope of glory.* (Col. 1:26, 27)

17

It is acknowledged that Paul wrote this letter somewhere between A.D. 60 and 80. That would have been about twenty-seven to forty-seven years after Jesus' ascension. So the words ages and generations clearly indicate that he was not talking about Jesus, but about something that both preceded and indwelled Jesus.

This "something" we interpret to mean the God idea of perfect man that is enfolded in *every* person. It is this universal idea of perfect man in every person that makes each one of us a member of the species we call man, just as it is the universal idea of a rose implanted in *every* rose seed that makes it a member of the rose species, and not a lilac or a cucumber.

This is not only a logical interpretation of Paul's classic statement: *Christ in you, the hope of glory,* but it also makes good common sense. For everything there is, there must be a basic idea, an invisible pattern, which gives the thing its character, its form, its uniqueness. We are no exception. The prototype idea of perfection is enfolded in everyone, and Paul labels it the "Christ." This is your hope of fulfillment of the tremendous potential enfolded in the species, man—God's highest creation.

At a seminar Dr. Ira Progoff referred to this same idea of the Christ in you as the "organic process" in man. He chose the word *organic* because in its precise definition, it means simply "growing." You may think of a plant when you hear the word *organic*. But it doesn't necessarily refer to plants; it can be used to describe anything that grows, as distinguished from something that is static.

The Christ idea in you is a "growing thing." It operates much the same as the idea of an oak tree that is implanted in every acorn. The invisible idea of an oak tree in the acorn is the creative intelligence that converts the chemicals in the earth and water into the complex and perfect pattern of growth toward a mature and beautiful oak tree.

Even so, it is the Christ idea in you and me that converts the raw materials of our lives—our environment, our thoughts, our reactions, our feelings—into a process of growth toward spiritually mature and perfect individualizations of the universal idea of perfect man.

Somehow the term *organic process* gave me a clearer perception of the Christ in me. Heretofore we may have thought unconsciously of the perfect Christ in us as being a static thing, an area of perfection hidden away someplace in our consciousness, our inner being. But the Christ isn't static. It is dynamic, or organic, in that it grows in us. It "grows" us!

You may say, "If there is only one idea of perfection, and that idea is implanted in every person, does that mean that when we are fully matured spiritually, mentally, and physically, we will all be the same?"

No, this is not the case any more than every rose or every oak tree is the same. They all spring from the same universal idea of an oak tree or a rose, but each is an individualized expression of that idea. Each one is beautifully, uniquely different and individual.

So each of us has his own uniqueness, his own individuality. Jesus completely expressed the Christ, and He opened the way for us to do the same. Jesus was, as He called Himself, our Elder Brother. The elder brother in the family always experiences things first. He is the first of the children in the family to ask to be allowed to drive the family car, the first to face the bewildering and sometimes frightening prospect of entering kindergarten, and later high school and college. His example somehow makes it easier for the second- and third-born. If the eldest received permission to drive at sixteen, the second-born almost takes it for granted that the same goes for him. He knows nothing of the pain and problems that the eldest son may have had in breaking through the arguments and perhaps stubbornness of the parents.

In a spiritual way, Jesus is our Elder Brother. He broke the ground for us. He is our trailblazer. He learned, practiced, and fulfilled the laws governing the growth of the Christ in man. And He taught us how to accomplish what He accomplished.

I feel that this idea of Jesus Christ as our loving example is explicit in His words: *"Truly, truly, I say to you, he who believes in me will also do the works that I do; and greater works than these will he do, because I go to the Father."* (John 14:12)

It isn't easy to perceive the concept of the Christ as tangible, because we are dealing with an intangible, invisible "something." How do we describe something that we can't see, hear, or touch?

We can start by realizing that within each of us there are several "selves." For instance, there may be a self that shows when we say cutting or sarcastic things. Although we may recognize that we have such a self, we are rather ashamed of it and try to keep that self hidden.

Many of us have a frightened self that shows itself when we are called on to face a new experience, such as traveling in an airplane for the first time, or driving alone to a far city. Again, we may not like that self, and try to keep it hidden from others although we know that it exists.

These various selves in us are invisible, intangible, in the same way that the Christ self is invisible and intangible. But let's see if we can draw these various selves out and deal with them in a positive way.

Say to your self, "Who is sometimes very sarcastic and critical?" To bring this self out more, think back to some time when you criticized something or someone, or made a cutting remark. Then ask your self again, "Who is sometimes sarcastic and critical?" And you may hear something within you say, a little meekly perhaps, "I am."

Do the same with the frightened self. Say, "Who is the one who panics inwardly when he must face a new experience?" And you may hear or feel something in you weakly reply, "I am."

Now . . . are you ready to hear the Christ in you? Say to your self, "Who is willing to overcome this frightened self and this unloving self, and walk upright, unafraid, confident?" And you will hear the Christ self within you shout, "I AM!"

Say again, "Who is willing to be undaunted in his faith and meet all life's experiences victoriously?" And from the depths of your being will come the ringing answer, "I AM!"

If you should become confused and nervous about what to do in a present situation, first ask your self very frankly, "Who is confused and nervous about this situation?" And you may hear a bashful, "I am."

Then say: "But who is one with God, the Source? Who is undaunted in faith that God will guide him safely and successfully through this experience?"

Listen, then, to the Christ in you answer, "I AM." Then relax and let that self of you do its perfect work.

Jesus taught that the kingdom of God is at hand, even within you. If this is so, it seems reasonable and right to get acquainted with your inner self, and to choose to follow that Christ self in all that you do. The Christ self is not some isolated, static something within you; it intermingles with all phases of your life, if you but have the eyes to see it and the intuition to recognize it.

You and I appear to have an outer life and an inner life. Your outer life is easy to observe, recall, and draw lessons from. Your outer life consists of physical things, such as changing from one job to another, moving to a new home, the death or illness of a friend, and so on.

But your inner life, how you have felt, how you have reacted mentally or emotionally to the procession of events in your life—this is not as easy to observe, recall, and draw lessons from! The inner life seems so fleeting, so subtle, so intangible, so quicksilverish. Yet it is just as real as the history of your outer life. In fact, it alone is real because it is the real *you*.

In a sense, outer events and circumstances are only the backdrop against which the real action of your life takes place. These things do not happen to a robot; they happen to a living, growing, maturing, developing inner you.

Your physical body continues to change, and all sorts of things may happen to it. But the inner you, the nonphysical you, the you that is basically spirit—an emanation of the one universal Father-Spirit, God—does not undergo change. It is this you that we are interested in in the spiritual life.

Within you—along with your past memories, all the beliefs you have accepted about yourself, all your self-constructed inhibitions—is the Christ. Paul's teaching of *Christ in you, the hope of glory* is still a mystery to many. We need to grow to the understanding that we have a seed idea of perfect man in us, just as an apple tree has to have the God idea of a matured and perfect apple tree invisibly enfolded in the original seed from which the tree grew. Within the inner you is this God seed of perfect man, the Christ: *Christ in you, the hope of glory.*

The purpose of this God seed individualized in you is to direct and guide, to "grow" you, the inner you, into perfect fulfillment, perfect expression of your spiritual potential.

How do you cooperate with this divine seed, with the Christ in you? In Unity we suggest several ways, and we are always looking for more. One way is to affirm the presence of the Christ within. A prayer affirmation that Unity students use is:

The all-knowing Mind of Christ is in me. I think clearly, I know intuitively, I act wisely, calmly, and confidently. I am grateful!

Here you are acknowledging the very real presence of the Christ within, your hope of glory, and becoming sensitive and receptive to its influence and direction.

Another way to begin to recognize the Christ within is to delve into the unfolding pattern of your inner life to discern the direction in which the inner Christ seed wants you to grow. Go apart to some quiet place with a pencil and notebook. Recall those times in your life that you would call "stepping-stone" experiences, or events or circumstances that greatly changed the direction of your life. When you have listed these experiences, you may receive a new and interesting view of the direction of your life. Take these experiences one at a time; go deep within yourself to remember how you felt, what you thought about, what your aspirations were, what real overcomings you were making. You may wish to write these thoughts in

25

your notebook and see what they seem to tell you about yourself, about your life. You will get a clearer picture of the direction in which your indwelling Christ has been leading you. Perhaps you will see how you may have gotten "off course," and you may want to consider how you can get back onto the path of your natural inner desires and talents and goals.

During this process, it may come to you what your strong points really are, and that they grow and unfold as you unfold spiritually. There is more to you than the thoughts going through your mind at the present moment. In meditation and contemplation you can rediscover the past "inner you" and lay it out in front of you on paper. Then you will find that your personal inner directive intelligence, the Christ, will speak to you as spontaneous insight, as *knowing,* and you will receive right direction through recognition of your inner Christ potential.

The Indwelling Christ

Indwelling Christ—The Son of God or spiritual nucleus within each person. . . . Each man has within himself the Christ idea, just as Jesus had. Man must look to the indwelling Christ in order to recognize

> *his sonship, his divine origin and birth,*
> *even as did the Savior. (Charles Fillmore,*
> *The Revealing Word)*

The concept of the indwelling Christ can be difficult to grasp. It slips through the fingers of the intellect when you try to tie it down in a neatly worded package. You can carefully study the words of great teachers such as Charles Fillmore; you can memorize Truth maxims, creeds, and statements of being; but still the concept of the Christ overlaps the bounds of the intellect.

Only in the inner depths of meditation, stripped of intellectual vanity, and with a simple, patient, childlike longing, does the seeking self find that mystery which cannot be reflected, bound, or confined by words.

The following meditation is but a guideline, "word hand holds"; the journey toward understanding the great mystery is yours to make.

Exercise

As you sit quiet and relaxed, think of the crown of your head as representing the Christ center or superconscious level of mind in you. Think of your forehead as representing the conscious level of mind in you. Think of the solar plexus as representing the subconscious level of mind in you. With your attention at the crown of the head, affirm silently: *The Christ indwelling is awakened in me.* Hold the thought briefly.

Bringing your attention to the forehead, affirm silently: *I am aware that the Christ indwelling is awakened in me.* Hold the thought the length of three easy breaths.

Dropping your attention to the solar plexus, affirm silently: *I am grateful that the Christ indwelling is awakened in me.*

The subconscious is the seat of the emotions, and you will "feel" a sense of peace in which are enfolded fleeting glimpses of understanding.

Now, in your meditation, proceed on faith—faith that there is in you and of you something that surpasses the intellect and outranks the limited, human self of you.

Even though you may feel you have experienced only the tiniest hint of the ultimate mystery of Christ in you, hang on to that hint with faith! Let go of worry, doubt, or strain, and affirm confidently: *I make my decisions under the direction of my own indwelling Christ.*

Feel a current of light emanating from the crown of your head and descending to below your feet as you affirm: *Through Christ in me I am inwardly renewed and wonderfully alive.*

Placing the attention first at the solar plexus, then at the root of the tongue, affirm: *Through the power of Christ within me, I meet all the affairs of my life confidently.*

Rest in the satisfying feeling that there is no need that you can have that has not already been provided for, as you silently know for yourself: *Christ within me is my unfailing source of supply.*

As you think of others in your life, and people the world over, affirm: *There is but one universal Christ individualized in and through every person. I behold the individualized, indwelling Christ in you, taking care of you in every needed way.*

Benediction Thought

I am grateful that I am becoming aware at deep levels of my being that God's only-begotten Son, the Christ, is awakening in me. I patiently wait, with a doubt-free and trusting mind, the ever growing understanding of the mystery of Christ in me.

III

The Spiritual Power of INdependence

In America, a group of settlers pioneered a new land. In the early days, they were dependent on Great Britain for many things: judges and courts, the legal system, soldiers for protection and law enforcement. It goes without saying that if this situation had continued, the colonies would have become progressively weaker and more dependent, while the parent nation would have become stronger.

When we depend on any person or condition or organization, that person or condition or organization gets more powerful as we become weaker and more dependent. We can find countless examples of this principle that total dependence on someone or something weakens us.

If a writer or an artist depends on ideas from

others, his own creativity becomes weak and fragile. His sense of dependency on the ideas of others becomes a kind of psychic pain to him. The same is true for schoolteachers, salesmen, doctors, people in every walk of life. The more we depend on other people's ideas or methods or opinions, the more we *have* to depend on others. This habit weakens and enslaves us. From this psychological slavery are spawned guilt, fear, insecurity, chronic anxiety, and illness.

Here is where the spiritual implications of this principle come in. If you think about it, you will come to the realization that you depend on outer things, conditions, and people for a great deal in your life. You depend on your paycheck, you depend on your stock portfolio, you depend on your job or the favor of people, the admiration of friends.

Whenever one depends totally on outer things, one gets feelings of emptiness, insecurity, fear. And it is because of that complete dependence on outer things and people that we often feel hemmed in, enslaved, or victims of circumstance. These feelings breed anger and hostility that in turn reflect in our physical bodies.

But we don't *have to* depend on outer things and people. The Bible gives us an alternative. If the entire theme of the Bible could be condensed into three words, they might be, Depend on God!

When we depend on God, the only part of us that is weakened is our vain little personal ego that was enslaved to the powerful suggestions of the outer world through its dependency on appearances.

When I say that we should depend on God only, I do not mean that we will not need food or money or a doctor's skill, or any of the other things that may be necessary for existence in this physical world. I mean that we must depend on God, the unfailing Source, the one unlimited Intelligence, to guide, supply, strengthen, and heal us. We do not need to question the means whereby this will be done; we do not need to doubt. We need only become totally dependent on what people through the centuries have accepted to be the highest, greatest, mightiest power in the world—God.

Where do we find God? Do we find Him in the sky or under an altar in a church? No, we find God in the secret place of the Most High, right within us!

When the time comes that we have had enough of being afraid, bored, tense, angry, emotionally drained, and we seek to break our dependence on the outer world of things and people that has brought us to this state, we must declare our *inde-*

pendence. We must learn to depend on the inner realm of the kingdom of God, which Jesus located within us.

The decision to become spiritually independent must be carried out in the everyday experiences of our lives. And this may not always be easy. It may entail a type of battle, even mental pain and psychological hardship. It may be painful for a time when we throw a crutch away; but unless we do, we will be enslaved to it for all time.

For instance, we will have to analyze the motives behind many of the things we do. Does our reason for doing something spring from fear of, or dependence on, outer conditions or people? Many times the sly personal ego will cleverly conceal the real motive and let us think we are doing something for an altruistic reason, when the real motive may be greed, ambition, or the seeking of power over others, all of which derive from a sense of separation from God and a dependency on outer conditions.

True faith in God has to be dependence on God. Total dependence on God means giving up depending on people, circumstances, conditions, and things. Total dependence on God brings peace of mind, calmness of mind through which we can plainly feel the inclination, the guidance, of God's Spirit from within us.

33

Through total dependence on God, or *inde-pendence*, we fulfill our potential, for only the wis-dom that is so much greater than the intellect can know the divine order and divine timing for grow-ing into glorious fulfillment according to the unique pattern of our individual being.

Try meditation. Try turning away from the outer distractions that fooled you into thinking they were "life," and that to be without them would be boredom and pain. Get acquainted with the inner side of life. At first it may seem strange, and you may long for the outer distractions. Your outer-oriented ego will cause you to procrastinate and make excuses to avoid meditating. Yet through meditation, you find that you can wake up from the spell that appearances have cast over you.

Although some popular approaches to medita-tion avoid the use of religious terms, and hereby are perhaps more acceptable to certain academi-cally oriented portions of society, the fact is that meditation is the kind of prayer taught and prac-ticed by Jesus of Nazareth.

When Jesus went into the hills alone to pray, He sought in inner silence to experience a dia-logue or communion with that universally present power that is called God. This is meditation.

When Jesus was asked how we should pray,

He gave us the Lord's Prayer as a meditation structure. Just as handholds are used in climbing, the phrases and sentences of the Lord's Prayer provide what we might call "mindholds" for going within to deeper layers of understanding, more intense realizations of God's nearness and our oneness with God. This is meditation.

If you are new to meditation, there is one premise that you must accept, for all that follows rests on this premise. Whether you are religiously oriented or not, this premise is so logical that you won't find it difficult to accept. The premise is: there is a universal, transcendent intelligence that originated and stands behind all that is.

Here is the self-evident logic of that premise. When you see a manifestation of intelligence, it necessarily follows that there must be an intelligence that caused that manifestation.

For instance, if you were exploring an uncharted jungle and came across a deserted village, you would know that the crude huts, because of their very existence, were incontrovertible proof that some intelligent life had caused this manifestation of intelligence.

This same principle may be applied to outer space. The planets and the precise orbits in which they travel can be compared to the village huts in our previous example. They are forms or manifestations of intelligence, and therefore their very existence is self-evident proof that a previous intelligence caused the manifestations.

We call this causative or originating intelligence God, and it is this that we seek to contact and experience in meditation. Jesus called this causative and all-potential dimension the kingdom of God, and He located it within man. We gain access to this kingdom through meditation.

Meditation enables us to act instead of just react to life. We sometimes seem to be automatic reacting machines, much like robots with a panel of buttons that is exposed and accessible to anything and anyone. When a certain button is pushed, we give a certain response. People who push these buttons of ours are called "motivators" because they try to motivate us to act. Madison Avenue is the term we use to single out the advertising motivators. These are skilled and clever individuals who know that words like *free* and *new* can motivate the masses. They know also the subtle ways to push the "fear" button to get us to respond in desired ways.

But Madison Avenue isn't the only outer motivator; actually, everybody we meet has access to our "buttons" and uses them, consciously or unconsciously. For instance, when someone says something nice to you, you react by feeling good.

If the next person says something critical about you, you respond by feeling deflated, hostile, or defensive. If you are unexpectedly forced to wait fifteen minutes past the appointment time that was reserved for you weeks ago, you may automatically and compulsively react with impatience or inner anger.

Think about it. Go through a typical day in your life. Ninety percent of the time you do not control your response; you automatically respond the way the outer stimulus, the outer motivator, tempts you to respond. The motivator can be a person, an event, or a circumstance; it can be a phone call, a piece of burnt toast, a drop in the Dow-Jones, or the tone of your boss' voice.

Meditation will give you back to yourself. The buttons are still exposed, but when the motivator—be it a person, an event, or a condition—pushes a certain button, the response is not necessarily automatic and predictable. There will be a delay while the suggestion of the outer stimulus goes to that center of calmness you have developed through meditation. There the inner light of understanding guides you in determining a right and wise response. And only then do you respond.

It is a whole new world when you learn how to act instead of merely react. You will realize how much control over your life you have given to outer conditions and people. Many of your problems will immediately disappear when you take back that control and act from your own free choice with the guidance of infinite Intelligence.

Then you will experience true freedom. When you automatically and compulsively react to outer conditions and people—the motivators, the manipulators, the button-pushers—you are in bondage to them. If a certain person or event or condition always makes you upset or angry or nervous, you are in bondage to that person or event or condition. Only when you consciously choose how you will act are you truly free.

It may help to think of the phrase, "Stop, look, and listen." When an outer motivator, whether person, event, or condition, pushes one of your buttons and you feel an automatic response arising, *stop, look* (that is, calmly look at or examine the response that wants to come forth automatically), *listen:* acknowledge that an inner light is revealing whether that response is right or wrong, thus inclining you to a right response. Turn within in a moment of meditation and become truly *in*dependent.

Meditation, true independence, is the key to the spiritual life. The spiritual life is truly what all people are seeking, whether or not they are consciously aware of it.

The inner Self is seeking the spiritual life because man *is* a spiritual being. The first chapter of Genesis states that man is created in the image and after the likeness of his Creator, God. If this statement is accepted as valid, it follows that there is that in man and of man that is Spirit, for God is Spirit.

Man as a spiritual being is expressing through a physical body, and we call this expression a human being. It is true that man is a human being, but it is also true that there is that in man and of man that transcends the human-beingness.

Living from the basis that you are *only* a human being is living a half-life. There is an inner, gnawing sense of incompleteness, of emptiness, of something vital that seems to be missing from our awareness.

Aware of this inner emptiness, and yet unaware that it is caused by a lack of understanding of our spiritual nature, we seek to fill the emptiness, or perhaps escape from it, by continually seeking outer excitements and stimulations to keep our minds and feelings busy.

For many people, the most nerve-racking experience in the world is to have nothing to do. We may read a paper we are not really interested in, or call someone on the phone just to pass the time, or go to a movie, or look for some activity—any activity—rather than have nothing to do except face that inner emptiness.

We may decide that this sense of incompleteness, this dissatisfaction, this inner insecurity, can be fulfilled by some outer condition. We may believe that if we were wealthy we would be happy and fulfilled; if we were famous and popular we would be happy; if only we had the power to make people do what we wanted them to do, or to shape conditions so that they were favorable to us, then life would be serene.

Yet we have seen ample proof that great wealth doesn't guarantee happiness, nor does fame, nor power. We also know that no matter how we may try to fill every moment with some kind of outer excitement, the emptiness is always there. And because outer excitements tend to lose their novelty, their power to sustain our interest, we must continually find new and more stimulating things to do.

Right at this point is where the teachings of Jesus come in. Look within, Jesus teaches. Go within, He urges. The kingdom of God, the home of the spiritual part of you, is within you! And going within is meditation.

Through meditation a whole new world opens up to you. You are no longer a slave to the outer world of sensations and excitements; you no longer need its stimuli to make you feel alive.

This doesn't mean that you renounce the outer world. The fact is, you enjoy it even more because you are not bound by it, dependent upon it. You can take it or leave it alone. You are free. You are in the world, but not *of* the world.

Not everyone is ready for the meditation experience. Many are so enmeshed in, entranced (hypnotized) by the outer world of effects and by the obviousness of their human nature, that they cannot and will not conceive of a realm that cannot be described in books or measured with scientific instruments, but can only be "experienced." And who are we to blame them? For long years we too may have searched in the outer; we too were so sure that someday we would find the pot of gold at the end of the rainbow.

But for you who want to strike out into a new country (the "promised land"), let us walk together on our inward quest. The following suggestion is called a "Dis-identification Exercise" and may help to guide us on the way.

The purpose of this exercise is to "dis-identify" your basic sense of "I" from the contents of your consciousness. As you learn to do this you are able to observe the contents of your mind—the thoughts, feelings, pictures, and so forth—objectively, dispassionately. Disidentification is not meant to eliminate thoughts, feelings, desires, and other psychological states. Let them arise; but instead of entering into them, or emotionally experiencing them, calmly observe them.

The next step is to seek the realization that the light of Truth is shining through the lens of your basic sense of "I" to impart understanding, wisdom, and guidance concerning what you are observing.

Make yourself comfortable, close your eyes, and relax. Then think to yourself: *I have a body, but I am not my body. My body is a wonderful, God-designed instrument through which I express, but I am not my body. Sometimes my body is tired, but the "I" that uses my body cannot be tired. My body may only transmit to the "I" of me a sensation of tiredness. After a while it will transmit a sensation of vigor or non-tiredness; my bodily sensations change and come and go, but my "I" remains ever the same. I bless my body and I am grateful for it.*

Next, think to yourself: *I have emotions and desires, but I am not my emotions and desires. They are psychological states that come and go, while my sense of "I" remains constant. I recall a time in the past when a state of anger held sway in me. It is no longer there. The state of anger has gone, but the "I" that experienced it is here now and always.* Think of desires in the same way; they come and go. You may say, "I fervently desire a dish of ice cream!" But the "I" of you doesn't desire it. What happens is that the desire born out of many past experiences of pleasantness associated with ice cream arises into your field of consciousness and you attach or identify your "I" with it and believe you desire ice cream. You do have desires and emotions, but you are not these desires and emotions. You have the ability to observe, control, accede to or deny them, as you choose.

Next, consider your thoughts. You have thoughts, but you are not your thoughts. William James defined consciousness as a *stream of thoughts.* Your thoughts stream through your mind in an endless procession. One train of thoughts links onto an associated train of thoughts. You may start with thoughts about a past conversation and end with thoughts about an episode in your childhood. Your thoughts come and go, but the observer, the "I" remains constant.

Then ask yourself, "What am I, then? What is left when I see that I am not my body, I am not my emotions and desires, I am not my intellect and thoughts?" What is left is a center of awareness.

You are that center of awareness, that center of self-consciousness, that center of power. From this center of awareness you have the authority to observe, direct, and wisely control and use the various emotions, desires, thoughts that come and go. Identified with your body or your emotions, you become their slave; disidentified from them, they become your servants to direct rightly and wisely.

Even the first time you practice this exercise, you will receive understanding beyond any of the words you speak or read. You will become aware of insights that you never read in a book. Then, the more you practice this exercise in disentangling your real Self from the clutter in your consciousness, the more you will gain mastery over the contents of your consciousness and the less you will be enslaved to the outer world.

Meditation is an inward quest. It is like exploring a new country; it is like launching into inner space. We need tools, instruments, gear, just as those who explore outer space do. This disidentification exercise is one such tool, one such instrument. Meditation techniques are merely structures, scaffolding, tools to help you to get in touch with the Father within, to contact the growth process within that is seeking to fulfill itself in you and through you and as you.

In time you will see that conditions have no power over you. Only God has power; and because of your oneness with God, because of your "child of God" nature, you are privileged to be a channel of that infinite power.

You will not leave the world through meditation, or begin to hate the world; you will have overcome the world's power to control you through hypnotizing you into thinking you are dependent on the world.

Think about it. Take time to turn within and investigate the advantages and possibilities of declaring your *independence*. Learn to depend completely, moment to moment, day to day, on the wisdom and guidance originating from the Spirit of God within you.

INdependence

What influences or determines your mental and emotional responses from hour to hour and day to day? Is it outer conditions, other people's opinions, or is it the light of Truth within you?

In meditation, you learn to be influenced by the light of Truth, to rely on it for support and aid. You learn to depend not on luck or the favor or praise of people, but on the wisdom and guidance of the Spirit of truth within you.

45

Think of your "I," the unchanging, permanent factor of your personality, not as a mirror that faithfully reflects the anger or resentment or fear suggested by outer appearances, but as a lens through which the light of Truth shines into your consciousness to impart wisdom, understanding, and right action.

Exercise

Know that this moment, the *open now,* has two ends: one opens into your outer world of effects, the other opens into the corridor of consciousness that leads to the allness of God. Know for yourself: *I now focus my awareness inward to the light of Truth. I bask in the light of God within me as a sunbather basks in the warming rays of the sun.*

Let the light of Truth shine into the deepest reaches of your subconscious to melt away all limited beliefs, all compulsive feelings resulting from forgotten negative experiences. Sit quietly and observe the thoughts that arise in your mind; through nonjudgmental observation, meaning and understanding are revealed. Affirm: *I am strong in the Lord; His Spirit works in me and through me. I know what to do and I do it.*

It does not surprise us when a physician's therapy corrects an unwanted physical condition—we *expect* this to happen. In meditation, focus the healing light of Spirit on your physical body and don't be surprised; *expect* the infinitely powerful life energy of God to correct, heal, and renew your body as you affirm: *I am strong in the Lord and in the power of His might. His Spirit heals me, mind and body.* Then relax and truly let go.

Adequate supply begins with a right attitude of mind. While facing the fact of lack or insufficiency, it may seem difficult to hold to faith in God as the source of your supply. You must try to disregard the appearances, or at least know that they are only temporary, and affirm: *The Spirit of the Lord adjusts and prospers my affairs now, and I am grateful!*

Benediction Thought

Now I go forth into my environment in a spirit of independence. I calmly observe events and experiences and look to the light of Truth within me for a correct response. The Spirit of the Lord goes before me, making my way safe, joyous, and successful, and I am grateful!

IV

In Tune with the Divine Vibration

Words hold secrets. When we look deep within a word to the idea it represents, it seems to release all kinds of ideas into our minds.

Take the word *charm*. We say, "What a charming room," or "He (or she) has such a charming personality." When we hear the words "charm school" we think of a place where young women are taught to walk erectly and gracefully, where they learn to bring out the attractive best in themselves.

Let's look at the idea at the heart of the word *charm*. It means "to subdue or overcome by some secret power; also, to attract irresistibly." We can see that this word can be used in a much wider sense than just to describe a particularly gracious room or a magnetic personality.

The moment our minds glimpse the words, "to

subdue or overcome by some secret power," we may think of the power of God. Surely the power of God is capable of subduing and overcoming every seeming obstacle, every apparent threat to our security.

You might stop to ponder the word *secret*. "The power of God is not a secret power," you might say. Yet the word *secret* doesn't necessarily mean something that is purposely kept hidden; it merely means something that is presently concealed. We say the ocean depths hold many secrets. I think, too, that there are many secrets about the power of God within us that are yet to be discovered.

Most of us will agree that there is a spiritual power within us, a power that is capable of subduing and overcoming the problems and challenges that come into our lives; this is the very power of God.

The question is, how can we contact and release this power? It seems that the main purpose of Jesus' ministry was to teach individuals how to contact and release the power of God within them!

Jesus came not only to reveal that there is a God; people already knew and acknowledged that. He came to teach that the God they acknowledged and believed in was not a personality separated from them, nor was He a presence dwelling behind the veil in the Holy of Holies at Jerusalem or any other place. Jesus taught that God is Spirit. God, as Spirit, is universally present and indwells each individual. " . . . *the kingdom of God,*" Jesus said, *"is in the midst of you."* (Luke 17:21)

Paul correctly interpreted Jesus' teaching when he wrote to the people of Corinth: *Do you not know that you are God's temple and that God's Spirit dwells in you?* (I Cor. 3:16)

When Jesus' seventy disciples went to carry the Gospel, the good news, to the people, they found that they could contact and release tremendous power to heal, to cast out demons, to meet courageously and overcome any danger that might confront them.

And what was the good news they carried to the people? It wasn't the book we now call the New Testament of the Bible, because the New Testament had not yet been written. The gospel they carried to the people was the teaching of Jesus that God is Spirit and that God's Spirit indwells us, and that through contacting and releasing the power of God's indwelling Spirit, healing is accomplished, danger is overcome, and our needs are abundantly fulfilled.

Somehow, through the centuries, this original

purpose and meaning of Jesus' teachings has become obscured, hidden. The power of God in us has remained a secret. Christianity as an institution or organization has grown to tremendous proportions, but Christianity as a teaching—Jesus' teaching of God as Spirit and God's Spirit indwelling us as an irresistible power to overcome and subdue all obstacles—has been suppressed, concealed, almost forgotten.

Here is a way of contacting or tuning in to this heretofore "secret" power of God within you. Basically, it is a matter of taking your attention off the apparent facts of any problem before you, and for a time focusing your attention on the unseen reality of the presence and power of God.

Tuning in on the secret power of God is placing your thoughts in tune with the all-powerful, everywhere present, all-wise Mind of God. To illustrate, suppose there are two pianos in a room. If you strike an "A" note on one, and then go and look within the other piano, you will find only one string vibrating—the "A" string. This means that a vibration emanating from the first piano has an actual and audible effect on another string that is tuned to the same vibration.

Now think of God (and all the spiritual resources and attributes of God) as a universal "A" vibration, so to speak, a specific vibration that is

51

eternally filling every part of creation—every mind, every cell, every atom. When we are consciously attuned to the "God vibration," through a positive change in our thinking, we will automatically experience definite, concrete, tangible evidence of that attunement in every area of our lives.

Thus Paul's statement is entirely logical: *. . . be transformed by the renewal of your mind . . . .* (Rom. 12:2) This teaching is the idea behind Jesus' words: *"But seek first his kingdom and his righteousness, and all these things shall be yours as well."* (Matt. 6:33) Seek first to get in tune through your thinking, and effortlessly, abundantly, all that you ask or need shall be yours.

Now, how do we go about attaining this attunement? Let's use a hypothetical problem to demonstrate. A businessman has been studying Truth principles and trying to practice them. One day an opportunity is opened to him to obtain a big contract that could lead to a tremendous expansion of his business. However, there are several "ifs"—unknown and unknowable factors—involved. This is his first experience in big business, and he is understandably nervous, even afraid concerning it.

Here is how he spiritually "charms" the situation—how he subdues or overcomes all obstacles to his good and irresistibly attracts success.

First, he studies the facts as well as he can. God works through us, through our consciousness, and so it is up to us to be as knowledgeable about the facts of a problem as possible. But as he studies the facts and acquaints himself with as many aspects of the situation as he can, he also makes a definite move to get his mind in tune with the universal vibration of God, the good omnipotent.

He sets aside a quiet time to formulate a prayer statement, and then he uses this statement in times of meditation until it becomes more than just words—a conviction, a deeply rooted belief.

Here is an example of the kind of statement I mean: *I totally accept the belief that I am one with the infinite wisdom of God, and that God's wisdom is being focalized through my consciousness and into my life to establish divine order, divine timing, and success in this situation. I am grateful!*

In this way, he is attuning his thinking to the God vibration. By the very nature of the universe, there will be a corresponding vibration or tangible manifestation of God, the good, in his specific situation. He finds fear leaving him, for God is his partner.

Adapt this spiritual prayer technique to your

own problem. Gather all the facts you can about the problem; don't try to hide from the problem, and don't be afraid of it.

Then make up a definite statement of belief about the situation which acknowledges your faith that a higher power, the power of God, is working in the situation. Be sure to add the spiritual catalyst: *I am grateful.* Then translate that statement of belief into total acceptance in your mind by repeated meditation on it and repeated affirmation of it.

Two qualities of mind are needed in this process: *patience* and *faith.*

Patience is a quality of mind that is essential to spiritual unfoldment. It may admittedly be difficult to develop, but without it we make little progress in learning to attune ourselves to the beneficent forces and laws of God.

Patience is something you cannot buy. It cannot be inherited. It cannot be given to you in any way. Patience is an attitude of mind that you must develop and nourish until it becomes an established, automatic, effortless response in the face of problems that seem to require a longer time-lapse for fulfillment than you would humanly prefer.

Patience is a sign of maturity, both emotional and spiritual. When a six-year-old can't have his ice cream right away, he may stamp his feet and go into a tantrum of impatience. An adult who is emotionally immature does not stamp his feet in a childish way; but when he wants something badly that he can't have right away, he may become sarcastic and bitter and may even make things difficult for those around him.

The person who is emotionally and spiritually mature knows that God is never late. He knows that God works through spiritual law, and that the operation of spiritual law is always a *process*.

In the fourth chapter of Mark, Jesus points out that all things must come through a process of growth: *"The kingdom of God is as if a man should scatter seed upon the ground, and should sleep and rise night and day, and the seed should sprout and grow, he knows not how. The earth produces of itself, first the blade, then the ear, then the full grain in the ear."* (Mark 4:26-28)

Here, very definitely and very clearly, Jesus is pointing out that the answer to our prayerful request, the fulfillment of our legitimate need, comes from the kingdom of God. But as it enters the kingdom of matter or form, it must conform to the law of growth. In other words, our full and complete healing, or the establishment of harmony in a broken human relationship, or whatever the answer to our need or good desire, is essentially a *process*. A process means that one thing follows the other in a lawful and necessary way.

We see this process that Jesus was talking about so clearly in all of nature, and we accept it with patience. If you plant a seed today, you do not expect it to be a full-grown plant tomorrow. But you know beyond a shadow of a doubt that it will someday be a full-grown plant, so you patiently wait, meanwhile watering and caring for it.

But somehow with our problems and challenges in life, we expect the answer to burst forth immediately. There are those who think that Truth should work like a magician who shouts, "Abracadabra," and *poof,* a bouquet of flowers appears or a rabbit comes out of a hat. It is my personal feeling that such people are getting both feet off the ground.

We need to keep one foot in heaven (the kingdom of God) and one foot on the ground (the material world). With the one foot in heaven, we acknowledge the existence of God and His ability to help us in every need. (Metaphysically, the feet symbolize understanding.) But with the other foot on earth, we realize that the translation of the answer from the kingdom of the unformed requires a process that may involve the factor of time. As Jesus said, " . . . *first the blade, then the ear, then the full grain in the ear."*

Let me hasten to add here that the time factor involved in translating the perfect answer that exists *now* in the kingdom of God to the formed answer in your physical world can be speeded up!

I am aware that there are instantaneous healings in many cases. But by "instantaneous" we really mean that the healing *process* was tremendously accelerated. The time factor, I am convinced, has to do with our consciousness. The more we can keep our faith centered on and in God, the more we can eliminate doubt and fear and all negative mental states from our consciousness, the more rapidly this process takes place. Here is where the importance of patience enters in again. When we are impatient, we are working against ourselves.

Impatience, as we all know from personal experience, is a definitely negative and destructive attitude of mind. We say, "He was fuming with impatience!" or "I got sick and tired of waiting." Believe me, these are not just empty metaphors! Impatience *does* "burn us up" physically and make the chemistry of our bodies "fume." Impatience actually *is* making us sick and tired. This destructive mental attitude storms through our field of consciousness and short-circuits the power of God, thus lengthening the time-lapse for our answer to come from the everywhere present kingdom of God into this four-dimensional world of length, width, depth, and time.

Impatience denotes a lack of faith. There are two kinds of impatience. One is the kind where we wish with all our heart that the seed we planted would hurry up and develop into the stalk of corn we so greatly desire. But we know that there is a necessary process involved, and so we busy ourselves with other things, and the impatience leaves us. The other kind of impatience is the kind that makes us so distraught and nervous that the first thing we know, we are digging up the seed to see if anything is really happening. We have our doubts, or we wouldn't dig up the seed to see!

This is the kind of impatience that we want to overcome, for it reveals a shallow faith. It has been said that our religion is what we believe to be true; if we really believe that there is a God who is all-powerful and all-wise, and who loves us and is working with us for our highest good, then although we may experience little pangs of impatience, wishing the goal were accomplished, in a deeper sense we are at peace and willing to let God work things out His way.

Sometimes we become impatient because we cannot see how some present experience can possibly have anything constructive to do with the answer to our problem. Here again is where faith and patience enter in. When these things happen in my life, I am always reminded of a picture puzzle I saw in a magazine years ago. It had tremendously magnified pictures of portions of familiar objects, such as a fork or a thimble. When I saw only the greatly magnified small portion of the object, it looked threatening and scary. I wondered what awful machine this could be a part of. But I remember my embarrassed feeling when I turned to the answer page, and saw that it was only the tine of a fork, or a portion of cabbage grater.

Life is like that. Sometimes when we are so immersed in the present moment of time, it is like looking at a blown-up portion of the overall answer to our problem. This small but greatly enlarged portion looks like anything but good; but if we can see the whole picture, or if we develop the faith to know that the whole picture is good even though the part we are seeing presently doesn't appear to be good, then we can lean back mentally and know that everything truly is in divine order.

Then we have the faith and patience to know that God knows what He is doing! This helps to accelerate the time factor and hasten the manifestation of our good.

Patience is essential to spiritual growth and unfoldment, for patience is proof of our faith as we wait for the answer to our need to come forth under an orderly process.

Whatever problem or challenge you may be facing at this point in your life unfoldment, remember: There is an answer, a perfect answer. The very existence of a problem means there is also an answer. The moment the problem came into existence, its answer also existed. Your answer exists now in the realm of the unformed, the kingdom of God. Seek God's help, get in tune with God. Remember that the answer comes from the unformed realm to the formed world as a process, so have faith; *be patient.*

The other quality of mind that is greatly needed in order to get in tune with the divine vibration is *faith.*

Our intellect tends to cancel out the operation of spiritual law with the words, the thought, the limiting belief, "Yes, but *how?*"

If there is one important thing for the serious follower of Jesus' teachings to learn, it is: *Don't ask "How?"* when you seek God's help in attaining the fulfillment of a legitimate need, or in achieving a deeply desired goal.

If you had never heard of electricity and someone told you to push a button on the wall so that there could be more light in the room, or asked you to turn a knob on what looked like a piece of furniture so that music would fill the room, and you said: "Yes, it would be nice to have more light, or to have music, but *how*? How is my pushing a button going to do this?" the other person would probably say, "Oh, for goodness' sake, don't stand there in the dark asking foolish questions—push the button!"

If when Jesus made the statement: " . . . *whatever you ask in prayer, believe that you have received it, and it will be yours,*" (Mark 11:24) you or I answered, "Yes, but *how*?" I wonder if He would answer, "Oh, for goodness' sake, don't stand there knee-deep in poverty or on the verge of a nervous breakdown asking foolish questions! Push the button—believe that you have received the answer and it will be yours!"

The intellect may survey the present facts and try to convince you that there is no way in the world for your answer to come, for you to attain that great desire. And every time the spiritual thoughts in you try to point out that, as Jesus said and as the Bible promised again and again, God *will* answer every need, the intellect may break down communication with the spiritual realm by insisting, "Yes, but *how*?"

There is only one way to handle this, and that is to appeal to the king of all your thought people, the will. Your will ultimately makes the choice of whether you take the advice of your intellectual thoughts or your spiritual thoughts.

Say within yourself, "I will to believe that my prayer request for the abundant fulfillment of my need is received! I have listened to my intellectual thoughts argue all the impossibilities of the situation. And I have listened to my spiritual thoughts with their fervent belief that the teachings of Jesus are true and valid and workable. I choose to go along with the spiritual thoughts, and from this time forward there will be no more 'Yes, but how?' in my thinking."

When you come to this decision, the spiritual law will begin to operate. Life will continue to unfold before you day after day; but as it unfolds, facts will begin to change in a new direction, in the direction of greater confidence, greater supply, greater faith, greater joy, greater inner peace.

Meanwhile, keep up your prayer work. Keep affirming, or "knowing" in meditation in frequent periods throughout your day: *I totally accept the truth that God is fulfilling this need in an easy, harmonious, and perfect way. I am grateful!*

Get into the habit of using "big" words in your prayer statements—words such as "tremendously successful," "amazing results," "delightful," "deeply satisfying." Don't limit the good that God wants to give you and is capable of giving you.

Jesus taught that according to your faith it is done unto you, so as you build your faith in God's fulfillment of your specific needs through your prayer statements, make that faith as unlimited as your imagination will allow.

Now someone may ask, "Does this mean that we don't have to do anything, that we just make the prayer statement in frequent times of prayer and then sit back and wait for something to happen?"

No, it doesn't mean that at all. What happens is that as life unfolds, as we enter one day after another, so to speak, we find that ideas for action steps will occur to us, and along with them will come the enthusiasm and the energy to take the action needed. Perhaps we will meet a friend who will give us an excellent lead. The list of situations and circumstances that *could* happen to start bringing about the fulfillment of our needs or desires is endless. We need only make our sincere prayer, including the statement that acknowledges and accepts the truth that the answer to our need already exists, and then watch how all things will begin to work together toward fulfillment.

The Bible teaches: *. . . faith is the assurance of things hoped for, the conviction of things not seen.* (Heb. 11:1) What do you hope for? Is it increased income, a strong, beautiful, healthy body, guidance in making an important decision, a way to help or understand someone close to you? Whatsoever you desire, only believe!

State your desire with faith and confidence, and meet each experience as it comes to you. You will see the pattern of your perfect answer emerging.

Thus you make contact that releases the ever-present power of God through you and into your life to bring forth the perfect answer. Thus you place your mind and your life in tune with the divine vibration. You are no longer meeting the problem alone—that is, with only your own knowledge, experience, and personal efforts. Instead, you are "hooked up" with a transcendent power that flows to you and through you, augmenting your own knowledge and efforts; using them, but also injecting a "secret power" that subdues and overcomes all obstacles and irresistibly attracts a right, perfect, and successful outcome!

"Father, I Am Grateful!"

Receiving the answer to your needs—physical, mental, or emotional—involves two mental movements. The first is asking, in which you define your need. The second is accepting, in which you articulate your faith that your request will be fulfilled. *" . . . whatever you ask in prayer, believe that you have received it, and it will be yours."* (Mark 11:24)

Saying, "Father, I am grateful," even as you define your need, fulfills the second movement; for you are saying, "I totally accept the belief that I do receive what I have asked." Gratitude sees and acknowledges the flower in the seed.

Exercise

As you begin your time of meditation, remember to relax. Loose and let go all tension of mind or body, knowing for yourself: *I am not my thoughts; I am not my emotions; I am not my desires. I am the changeless identity who says to my thoughts, "Come," or "Go." I now say to tension, "Go!" I now say to peace and stillness, "Come."*

Know for yourself: *I abide in the peace and stillness of an ordered mind.*

Whatever life holds for you as one hour and one day follows the next, know that you now make that inner contact which attunes you to the guidance of universal wisdom.

Affirm: *Father, I am grateful for light, wisdom, and understanding to meet all life's experiences victoriously.* This day, this hour, is brimful of blessings as you let the Father within guide you toward your highest good. *I will instruct you and teach you the way you should go.* (Psalms 32:8)

Know that you are in tune with the divine vibration, and feel it flowing through you as you affirm: *Father, I am grateful for life and strength flowing in and through me, healing my mind and body.*

Affirm for yourself: *Father, I am grateful for success and prosperity.* " . . . *it is your Father's good pleasure to give you the kingdom."* (Luke 12:32)

Joyously take time to give thanks for as many of your blessings as you can think of. And know for others: *Father, I am grateful that You fulfill in Your perfect way the needs of those for whom I pray. I loose and release them to Your loving care.*

Benediction Thought

I hesitate to withdraw from this peaceful time of meditation, but my hesitation is quickly overruled by an upsurge of eagerness to meet the experiences that lie before me with a freshly awakened consciousness of my attunement with God, the divine vibration. I am grateful!

V

Mind: the Master Power

Those who study the field of communication between people have found that most words have two meanings. First, there is the meaning as defined in the dictionary. Second, there is a meaning that each individual listener or speaker gives to the word. The dictionary definition stays much the same through the years. But the meaning to the individual differs according to his past experience with the word—how it was used in his presence, the feelings he experienced when the word was used. Because of this it is possible for a perfectly good word to take on a kind of taint for the individual, to become clouded with a personal meaning that many times obscures and twists the original dictionary meaning.

Such a word is *mysticism,* and its derivative words, *mystic,* and *mystical.* William James in his classic book "The Varieties of Religious Experience," writes: *The words "mysticism" and "mystical" are often used as terms of mere reproach, to throw at any opinion which we regard as vague and vast and sentimental, and without a base in either facts or logic.*

He then goes on to explain: *One may say truly . . . that personal religious experience has its root and centre in the mystical states of consciousness.*

But now let's see how the dictionary defines this seemingly maligned word. Webster says: *Mysticism: the belief that direct knowledge of God, or spiritual truth, is attainable through immediate intuition or insight and in a way differing from ordinary sense perception or the use of logical reasoning.*

In the light of this definition we must conclude that anyone who seriously follows the instructions of Jesus must be a mystic. Jesus taught that we must seek God within; that the kingdom of God is at hand, even within us. Understanding is not to be attained through books and teachers, but is imparted intuitively from the spirit of Truth within man.

Remember the words in the dictionary definition, "in a way differing from ordinary sense perception or the use of logical reasoning." Sense perception means, of course, gaining information through the channels of the five senses; in short, looking at the facts. Jesus teaches that we must look through or past the facts to the very real presence and power of the spiritual dimension of life.

Facts are effects. They are the results of previous causes. They can be compared to arrows that have been shot and are now sticking into the target. To deal exclusively with facts is foolish, useless, and frustrating. The wise person deals with causes, not effects. If the arrow misses the center, he doesn't wear himself out trying to pull it out; he takes more careful aim and shoots another arrow. In short, the wise person seeks guidance from the light of Truth within and initiates a new cause.

Christianity, as taught and lived by Jesus, is a practical religion, a realistic religion, and it is also a mystical religion. The results of living by spiritual principles are practical, but the process by which these results are obtained is mystical.

For instance, Jesus was a realist. He was practical, but He was also a mystic. The realist in Him saw five thousand hungry people; the mystic in Him provided the means to feed them. Throughout the three years of His ministry, we see example after example of His realism. Thousands came to Him for healing, for help of all kinds; with the eyes of a realist He looked on their troubles, and with the heart and mind of a mystic, He spoke the word that healed them and set them free.

This, then, is our goal: to be practical mystics. We do not want to retreat from the world and say, "Sickness, war, and trouble do not exist." But we want to know, "These things *do* exist; they are effects of previous causes." We can't change the effect—put a bandage on it, cover it up. But we *can* start a new cause, a more perfect cause, that will result in more nearly perfect effects.

And we do this by going back to First Cause, First Principle—God. We need to get our thinking and feelings aligned with universal Mind through meditative prayer. Then slowly, perhaps, but inexorably, the outer screen of effects begins to change.

This might seem to be too big a bite to take in regard to world problems of war, greed, dishonesty in high places, ruthless ambition. But we can apply the same principle to our personal lives to change them for the better; and in so doing we will be giving our candlelight contribution to solving national and world problems. We can resolve, "Let there be an end to war, anger, greed, dishonesty, selfish ambition, pride, and all the things that lead to ugly and destructive effects, and let them end *within me*."

Then look to the problems of your own personal world:

Here is a marriage that is going sour;

Here are teenage children who are causing their parents worry and anxiety;

Perhaps your job is in jeopardy; perhaps you are caught in a legal entanglement.

Young people might have problems of tension and anxiety about examinations at school, or about being accepted, loved, belonging.

Whatever your problem, you can begin by knowing there is an answer. A problem implies an answer, just as one end of a piece of string implies the existence of another end.

What would Jesus do if He had your problem? Don't avoid the question by saying that Jesus would never have a problem like yours. Perhaps not; but then, nobody else in the world has quite the same problem that you have. Jesus had His own problems, yet He went aside to pray, to meditate in order to solve them. He did not use the ritualistic prayer, reciting a memorized string of holy words put together by some church council in the dim past. Jesus went apart alone and in solitary, meditative prayer, had His dialogue with God.

God is here now with us just as God was with Jesus in Galilee. Meister Eckhart, the fourteenth century mystic, wrote: *God has spread His nets and lines out over all things, so that He may be found in any one of them and recognized by whomever chooses to verify this. . . . Man is not blest because God is in him, but in that he is aware of how near God is!*

You may ask, "How is meditative prayer going to change anything in the outer?" Outer things can be changed by prayer in a multitude of ways. It may be that you will *see* things differently. Parts of the so-called problem may take on new and different values. The light from within may reveal that what you thought was an insurmountable problem was really only a tempest in a teacup compared to the overall course and purpose of your life. Or it may be that touching the quiet depths within where the Spirit, your sense of I AM, merges and mingles with the universal Spirit of God gives you an inner calmness, a sense of patience, and in a moment of Truth, understanding bubbles up to the surface of your mind.

It may be that you receive immediate insight into yourself and your true motives. Many times the real cause of a problem is a selfish motive. Seeing and eliminating the selfish motive eliminates the problem. For instance, if a politician has an "ulcer-inviting" problem because he has not been able to get certain people to back him in what he feels is an important project, in meditation he might see how he had really wanted the success of the project to further his own ambition. Upon recognizing his real motive and knowing that personal ambition is a spinner of false promises, a liar, a tempter, he drops his intense personal hold on the project. Then, if it is really a worthwhile project and there is no longer a wrong motive behind it, it works out effortlessly. And if it wasn't really a worthwhile project, it fails. And who cares—it wasn't right anyway!

If things are at a standstill in your life and the more you push and sweat and worry and force, the worse they seem to get, go deep within yourself and ask God to check out your motive. If the motive is wrong, nothing works out right. Even if you force it to work out from a wrong motive, you gain nothing but guilt, sleeplessness, tension, and a sense of having to maintain the charade all by your lonely self.

If you can look at things from the standpoint of practical mysticism, you realize that to be practical or realistic means that we face our problems; we don't run away from them or fear them. To be mystical in our approach means that we can handle problems. We can approach them the mystical way through knowing that *the direct knowledge of God or spiritual Truth is attainable through imme-*

diate intuition or insight and in a way differing from ordinary sense perception.

In short, become quiet, turn within, seek understanding with all your heart and soul, and wait. We do acknowledge problems; we acknowledge the facts. But then we go on to place the emphasis on how to solve the problems by going past the facts to the spiritual realm, the realm of answers, of God.

When one is not aware of the positive power of the mind, it is easy to find things that are wrong with this world. At election times, the politicians look at all the things that are wrong and try to pick out the "hottest" issues, or issues that easily arouse an emotional response in people. It is a principle well-known to professional persuaders that an emotional response renders a person highly suggestible, and thereby easier to influence.

But we must remember where true reform begins. Does it begin by passing laws, or does it begin in the mind of the individual?

Certainly slums and poverty are bad, evil. What do we do about it? We could pass a law to tear down all slums and give all those who fit the poverty definition an annual income that would place them in a "middle-class" category.

This seems fine, but it is taking for granted that everyone in the middle-class category is happy, content, with no complaints or feelings of injustice being done them. Yet this isn't realistic. Middle-class people have all sorts of problems. They too may be unhappy, crusading for causes, worrying about money, trying to pay skyrocketing costs. What makes us think that eliminating the poverty category would make everyone happy, or be the answer to all problems?

Let's go further. If we think the middle class tends to blame all or most of its troubles on lack of money, let's eliminate the middle class, and make everyone millionaires. This too would be fine if it were true that millionaires are necessarily happy, secure, never bored, no complaints, contented residents of a material Shangri-la. But are they always? From my observations, I would say no. What do you think?

Reform begins in the mind of the individual. The fulfillment we seek is not to be found in or measured by material standards. We are all looking for the same thing, and it is available to each of us, no matter what our income or what kind of a place we live in. The person who lives in a basement in the slums and the person who lives on a luxurious estate have equal opportunity to turn within and be fed from the fount of wisdom, of understanding, of life, of power.

Something happens when you turn your allegiance around and give your loyalty to the creative Source of all things. The slum dweller will find his world of effects changing for the outer tends to reflect the inner beliefs and psychological states. The millionaire, too, will find his life becoming less complex and more simplified.

When the individual changes as a result of touching the inner springs of power and wisdom, his personal environment changes for the better. And as more and more individuals change, a mighty ground swell develops and we eventually find people changing, the world changing.

Try to envision a new category system: Instead of the "poor, middle-class, and rich" structure in which man receives his motivation to act, aspire, and accomplish from the outer, materialistic surface goals and values, there would be but two categories: those who look to and receive their motivation from within, and those who continue to receive it from outer values.

Let us think about this inner life. If we grant that there is something to this kingdom of God that Jesus said was not only right here at hand, but also within the individual, how do we go about getting acquainted with it? We start with God. We ask ourselves whether God is made in the image of man—that is, a superman sitting on a throne in a place in space called heaven—or whether God is Spirit—everywhere evenly present Spirit.

If we are to acknowledge that Jesus knew something of the nature of God, we must think in terms of God as Spirit. He taught that God is Spirit, and at no time did Jesus imply that God is a man on a throne in the sky. We realize that God *is* Spirit, and that the place where we contact this universal Spirit is within us. Now let's add to that some of the powers and characteristics that Jesus, the Bible, and individuals through the centuries have ascribed to God.

God is infinite wisdom. Let's remind ourselves that the word *infinite* means "lacking limits or bounds, endless, immeasurable." God's wisdom, then, is lacking in limits or bounds; it is endless, immeasurable. Surely this is far greater than the finest computer or the wisest man who ever lived.

Our logical thinking has now brought us to the point where we must conclude that within the individual there is a resource of wisdom that is greater than anything in the outer world—without limits or bounds. The next step is to *believe* this! We must not only accept it intellectually, but really believe it. Once we will to believe in the logical implications of Jesus' teachings, the next step is to depend on the guidance of that inner wisdom.

This may present a great obstacle. We have been so indoctrinated, programmed to depend on outer things—people, our job, our stocks, our government, our education—that this change of allegiance may be difficult. But we must make a start, we must try to redirect our dependence from outer things that are subject to change (or to use the Bible's metaphor, that are like grass that withers and dies) to dependence on the invisible, intangible but very real presence and wisdom of the universal Spirit that stands behind and within the formed universe.

The starting place is that sense of "I" that gives us an awareness of being. This is a point of radiation for a creative energy that lies back of it. When that point of radiation is aligned with this creative energy, or God, it becomes an outlet for all the powers and wisdom potential in that universal Spirit we call God.

When that central "I" is out of alignment with the creative energy back of it, the energy is short-circuited, we might say, into forming outer appearances, outer conditions that we call bad, evil, undesirable, or whatever other words we may use to describe the outer causes of our troubles and worries.

The way to get the central "I" of you realigned is to learn to love periods of solitude and prayer as much as you love television or playing golf or fashion shows or football. You will love the solitude of prayer or meditation once you get acquainted with the wonders and peace and beauty of that ideal "vacation spot" which is as near to you as you wish it to be.

As you get acquainted with your inner self and the vastness into which your inner self opens, you begin to see that your sense of "I" is like a pivot. It can turn outward and attach itself to worldly values, beliefs, opinions; or it can turn inward and attach itself to the flow of power and wisdom from the universal source of being.

As an example, your sense of "I" can contemplate the outer facts of the loss of a job, or of circumstances that seem to hem you in and keep you from being happy or getting anywhere in life, and it can attach itself to the discouraging and painful thoughts that arise from contemplating these disheartening facts. Or it can turn from these thoughts and contemplate the Truth that you, the central "I" of you, are a spiritual being, a spiritual entity. The central "I" of you is a point of radiation for the all-potentiality of universal Spirit or God.

Your central "I" can will or choose to say in effect: "You take over, God; You take over, infinite wisdom. I put aside all personal anxiety and worry." Anxiety and worry are only vanity anyway. Anxiety means that you are trying to do something all by yourself and are secretly afraid you can't do it, and you fear the world will find out that you are not so smart after all.

To verbalize these two contrasting sets of thoughts, the appearance-attached "I" says: "I am afraid; I am desperate. I am helpless and must find someone or some lucky circumstance to get me out of this." The thoughts of the God-attached "I" would be verbalized something like this, "I don't know what to do and I admit I don't know what to do. I depend on You, infinite wisdom, to motivate me toward right action, to direct me in the way that is best for me. Because I trust You, I am calm, serene, and unworried even in the face of these facts."

It is true that this is a complex world we live in and that it does seem to become more complex, confusing, and bewildering every day. But there is a way out; there is an answer. That answer lies in rightly understanding and using that nebulous, hard-to-pin-down-with-a-definition thing that we call *mind.*

There is a poem that defines mind as *the master power that molds and makes,* and says that man's environment is his *looking glass.* This is a thought-provoking idea. A looking glass is something that reflects the exact image of ourselves. If we stand in front of a mirror and get tremendously angry about something, the mirror reflects an image of a face contorted with rage, a frightening, ugly sight. The mirror isn't responsible for that terrifying image. It is merely reflecting what we give it.

Even so, our outer world—the problems, pressures, experiences that we face today—reflects the contents of our minds—the fears, hang-ups, beliefs, and reaction-patterns in our minds.

This is difficult to face; but until we face it we are going to continue to be like a bull in a china shop, charging around trying to get out, to escape, but only succeeding in causing more damage and hurting ourselves more and more. Every time we get angry, our environment responds with some sort of unhappy event, condition, or circumstance. We may say, "My anger is justified. What was done to me was mean, nasty, selfish, unjust." Still, if we look in a mirror when we are angry, the mirror gives us back an ugly, distorted, anger-ridden face. The mirror cannot say to itself: "This anger is justified, so I won't give him back an ugly, angry face. I will reflect a nice, pious-looking, angelic face because his justified anger makes him righteous and good." A mirror can't talk, nor can it judge. Neither can our environment talk or judge. It gives us back exactly what we give it.

Yet, how we make excuses for our responses to life, for our anger and fear and hostility and resentment! We say, "You can't blame me for get-

81

ting mad, can you?" or, "After all, I'm only human; I can only take so much."

First of all, we are not "only human." Is it not true that we are made in the image and after the likeness of God as is stated in the first chapter of the Bible? God is Spirit, and as His image-like-nesses we partake of God's spiritual nature. We are human, true. But something within us is Spirit, or spiritual. Therefore we cannot logically or truthfully say that we are "only human."

If we add, "I can only take so much," we are right! We can only take so much anger or hostility or hate, and then we blow up; we get sick physically or mentally. But who is giving us what we are taking so much of—the anger, hate, hostility? We are! We don't *have* to react that way; we are simply choosing to react that way. It may seem to be the easy way, for it appears to make us feel justified. However, it also tends to make us sick and miserable. What a price to pay!

Thought, then, is the tool, the instrument, the means whereby we direct the master power of mind and shape what we will—an environment of sadness, lack, trouble, or of joy, happiness, fulfillment, success.

How do we change our minds? How do we rightly use the instrument of thought to shape a new world, a new and better environment? Well, we can't change our minds in the past. The past is over and done. We can't change our minds in the future—it isn't here yet. We can only change our minds in the present moment. It is a good start to be able to say to yourself, "*Now* is the only time to change my mind and thereby change the looking glass of my environment!"

What you do in the *now* is wait—wait for an experience to come up that tempts you, invites you, entices you to react in an angry or resentful or jealous way, or to react with hate or revenge or smoldering impatience. When such an experience does arise, there is your opportunity to change! Your usual or habitual reaction would be to get impatient or angry or resentful or nervous. That is the "old" you. That is the you that is being reflected in the looking glass of your environment that you don't like, that you want to change. So this is where you walk the razor's edge. Do you give in and get angry, resentful, and remain unchanged? Or do you take control over that wrong feeling welling up in you and throw it out? You *can*, you know; you have that power. You are not your feelings. You *have* feelings, but you are not your feelings. You can invite feelings to stay, or you can dismiss them. The trouble with these wrong feelings is that they turn the tables on you. You are the master and they are the guests; but if you permit them to remain as guests too long, they take over your house. They become entrenched and you cannot easily get them out!

The first time you try to choke off a feeling of anger or resistance in your determined campaign to change your mind and thereby change your presently miserable environment, you may find it very difficult to do. Your unwanted guests will say to you, "This is different. You are justified in resenting his actions. Nobody would blame you for getting angry under these conditions." They can be very persuasive. They make it seem easy and logical and even seemingly right to respond wrongly.

But if you stand firm, and remain calm and unruffled, if you refuse to respond in kind to this anger-provoking temptation, you have really begun to change! If you pass the "razor's edge" (your moment of decision) successfully, you experience two results: you will feel a lot better than you thought you would—a lot better than that false feeling of being right and good and justified that you thought you got from "blowing your top"; and you will get a small but delicious taste of that feeling or quality that is called *mastery*. You will have exercised your authority as master of your house of the mind. The second pleasant result is that the outer circumstance that originally triggered your wrong response of anger or resentment will disappear, lose its sting, will retreat with its tail between its legs because it found no response in you. The only power it had to hurt you or frighten you came from *you*, from your own anger or resentment. You withheld that power, so the negative appearance had no power over you.

Wait once more for another irritating, upsetting, wrong-response-provoking experience to come. This one may be too much for you. You may react in the old way, getting very upset, hostile, filled with self-pity. But this experience can be useful. It can show you how subtle the temptation to think and act wrongly can be; and it can cause you to roll up your spiritual sleeves and say, "Try that again—just try that again. We'll see who wins this time!"

This brings us back to meditation. You can't change by strength of human intellect alone. But remember you are not only human. There is that in you, available to you always, that transcends your humanhood. Call it by whatever name you wish: God, the Father within, the Christ Spirit, or *"The true light that enlightens every man . . . . "* (John 1:9) And the way you contact this light or presence of the Father within you is in the quietness of meditation.

Underneath *every* noise you hear is silence.

Underneath and in between the words you are reading now is silence. Listen to, be aware of, seek to feel and enter into this universal field or ocean of silence. God is in the silence; God *is* the silence. Soon you will become aware of and express strength, understanding, an ability to stand calm in the face of the ups and downs of life that you never knew you possessed.

Meditation

Meditation is not "not thinking"; rather, meditation is "observing" your thoughts. Meditation is not "reading," not even reading the Bible or a Truth book. Rather, meditation is taking a statement or paragraph you have read and letting it speak to you through the thoughts that arise in your mind. Meditation is not gazing at a religious picture or decoration. Your attention is then on an outer stimulus. The spiritual "high" is counterfeit, for its motivating power comes from outside of you. Rather, meditation is closing your eyes purposely to avoid outer distractions, even religious symbols, so that your attention can be centered on the inner realm toward which the religious symbols point. Meditation is not for the purpose of finding relief from tension; rather, meditation is a way of forearming yourself so that you will not yield to the temptation of outer experiences that tend to make you tense or upset.

Exercise

Relaxation is a preliminary step in achieving a fruitful inner dialogue with God individualized in you. Therefore, relax the body. Quickly or slowly, as you feel led, relax and bless your body from your toes to the top of your head.

Now, with closed eyes, gaze forward and slightly upward. Be aware for a moment of your rhythmic breathing. You may sigh, and a pleasant "settling down" feeling will envelop you.

Soon thoughts will arise or "cross your mind." Where at first you may have seemed to be staring into grayish darkness (which is really the back of your eyelids), now these thoughts will capture the attention of your "I." This is the point where you want to learn to disengage your "I" from being enveloped by thought; to stand back and observe it objectively, without judgment, without emotions: " . . . *take every thought captive to obey Christ . . . . "* (II Cor. 10:5)

As you unemotionally observe thoughts that bubble up from within you, acknowledge that the light of Truth originating in the kingdom of light within you is shining through the lens of your "I" to shed light on the thought in mind to impart wisdom and understanding. *By wisdom a house is built, and by understanding it is established.* (Prov. 24:3)

In this part of your meditation time, you may wish to take a statement of Truth with you into the secret place of the Most High. In the silence there, let the idea within the words seep into the innermost depths of your being. *Take with you words and return to the Lord . . . .* (Hos. 14:2)

For guidance, affirm: *I am relaxed, peaceful, and confident. God inspires my thoughts, words, and actions.*

For healing, affirm: *I rest in the presence of God within me, and my body responds to the outpouring of His healing life.*

For supply, affirm: *I am relaxed, for I know that with God all things work together for good. All my needs are fulfilled.*

And know for others: *I am filled with peace and confidence as I relax in the realization that God is your help in every need.*

Benediction Thought

As I come to the close of this time of prayerful solitude, and again become exposed to the distractions, temptations, and demands of my outer environment, I take with me a still center of inner calmness that enables me to withhold a compulsive response and wait for and depend on guidance from the light of Truth within me. I am grateful!

VI

The Power of a Mental Image

In past chapters, we have been learning how to distinguish between the central "I"—the central "I AM" of our being—and the various moods, mental states, emotional states, and others that come into our field of consciousness. To illustrate, when a person says, "I am tired," he doesn't mean the "I" or "I AM" of him is tired. He really means that the "I," or his central identity, is experiencing and attaching itself to a feeling of tiredness in him. To prove this, we could tell that person that he had just inherited a million dollars, or that a loved one he hadn't seen in years was waiting outside for him, and immediately the tiredness would vanish. To be more exact, he would detach his "I" from the feeling of tiredness, and attach it to the feeling of joy and well-being that arises in him as a result of the good news. If you will think about this, you will see that the central "I" of him has not been tired. If it had been, it would remain tired in spite of the good news.

The central "I" or "I AM" of you is your spiritual center of identity. It is universal beingness, or God, expressing in, through, and as you. It is pure self-consciousness and cannot be tired, discouraged, sick, or in any other of the negative mental and emotional states we identify it with. This realization is an important first step in your exploration of "inner space" that we agree is the direction we need to take in order to catch up with the scientific advances in the outer.

Learning this first step has surely brought definite beneficial results in your life already. You have realized that your basic "I," or sense of beingness, is something apart from whatever mood or mental state you may be experiencing. And probably in a number of cases, you have been able to detach your "I" or your "self" from a negative mood and attach it to a more positive and beneficial mental state. The object of all this is not merely to isolate your central source of self-consciousness, your "I," but rather to learn how you can *choose* what you will attach it to. This, you see, is self-mastery! The Bible says: . . . *he who rules his spirit* [is better] *than he who takes a city*. (Prov. 16:32) Your "spirit" as used here

91

means your mental and emotional world with all its tremendous energies—energies that when properly understood, developed, and directed or ruled, prove to be infinitely greater than the nuclear energy of the outer world.

Let us think about one of the faculties or tools that your central "I" uses—the faculty of *imagination*. The point we are going to reach is that this central "I" of you can learn to *use* its faculty or power of imagination constructively to change outer conditions. The most significant thing about the imagination is that your subconscious mind—that powerhouse which shapes your outer circumstances and conditions—is as much influenced by the pictures you consciously select to throw on the screen of your imagination as it is by the actual things you experience through your senses in the physical world around you.

Your subconscious mind is a tremendously powerful servant (or perhaps we should say "helper" or "ally"), but it has one major limitation: it cannot tell the difference between something you are vividly imagining and something that is actually happening. For example, let's say that you are walking through a forest as darkness falls. Ahead of you is a moss-covered tree stump. However, in the fading light you imagine that you see the shape of a grizzly bear. How does the subconscious react? Does it discern the actual fact (a tree trunk) from the picture that is in your imagination, the picture you are mentally seeing? It reacts, of course, according to your mental image and starts your heart pounding, directs adrenalin to be poured into your bloodstream, and signals many other complicated chemical and physical changes to take place in you.

Knowing this truth about the subconscious mind, you can see how you can put your imagination to work in a positive way. For instance, if you had what is commonly called an inferiority complex, you would feel that you did not know as much as others, that you could not speak well in public, that you were a "nothing" and a "nobody," and that it took all of your energy just to keep yourself out of situations where people might discover how inferior you were. Such a feeling would naturally keep you from being a success, keep you from being the respected and sought-after person you would like to be.

If you know anybody with an inferiority complex, you know that it shows in many ways that may be unknown to that person. In the case of salesmen, they may even say the right words and try to appear enthusiastic; but if inside they are feeling that they will be lucky if they can even make their quota that month, somehow that feeling communicates to others. Yet in the light of what we have learned of the central "I" of our being and the mental and emotional states to which it attaches itself, we can see that the "I" of the person with an inferiority complex isn't inferior. The "I" could never be inferior; it is Spirit, and Spirit cannot be inferior.

A psychological state or a mental complex in the field of consciousness of this person has been built up through his mental and emotional responses to many life experiences. And the person is attaching his central "I" to this mental state; he is submerging his central "I" in this complex; he becomes it, and it becomes him.

Here is the spiritual therapy for overcoming such a limiting and crippling state of affairs. Find a quiet place and make yourself comfortable. Constructively use your imagination to help your body and mind relax. Remember, your subconscious, which directs the relaxing activity within you, doesn't know whether you are actually experiencing a thing or vividly imagining it. So, vividly imagine a quiet place, a garden, a favorite woodland scene. Feel the warm sunlight, hear the birds, perhaps even feel the bark of the tree you may be reclining against. You will soon feel relaxed, yet inwardly alert.

Now, say or think to yourself that the central "I"

or "I AM" of you is a center of pure self-consciousness that is flowing out from the one Source of consciousness—God. Start making pictures with your faculty of imagination. Picture this "I" of you, which is an expression of God's own Spirit, clothed in the garment of flesh which is you, or which you call your body. Or, if you are a salesman, you might try picturing yourself going into a prospective customer's office. See yourself going through the greeting and the presentation confidently and with supreme self-mastery. Picture the customer being pleased and signing the order for the amount of goods you lovingly, justly, and with his interest in mind have suggested.

See what is happening? The more vividly you picture your central "I" attached to or identified with a mental attitude of confidence and success, the more your subconscious mind accepts this as actually happening and tends to react that way in subsequent "real" situations.

You must be realistic. You may not get miracle results the first time, but you are on the way. Subsequently, you will feel more at home in your imagination. You will be able to make your mental pictures more vivid. As Aristotle pointed out so many centuries ago, virtue is only virtue when it is converted into action. To say you are a child of God is a wonderful statement; but you *become* a child of God in reality only when you *act* like one!

We all understand how difficult it is to act like a child of God when our "I" is submerged in a mental state of inferiority, selfishness, or fear of failure. Therefore, by using rightly our wonderful tool or faculty of imagination we can practice acting like a child of God in our meditation times; our subconscious will "pick up" the picture and soon we will be acting outwardly like the child of God we have always been potentially.

It is good to be mindful of the trouble we can bring upon ourselves by the wrong use of imagination. Many television commercials graphically picture the negative aspects of not using their products. These "visual suggestions" can become impressed on the subconscious mind. Have you ever had an insurance company representative quote you death-and-disaster statistics, with the subtle hint that these things could happen to you? There is no argument; we can't prove that these things will not happen, but sometimes we forget that the statistics don't *prove* that they will, either. Meanwhile, the suggestion may be planted. Suggestion is a form of hypnotism, and unless we truly "rule our own spirit" we can be easily manipulated. Watch the mental pictures your imagination produces. Censor out the negative pictures. Use your imagination to form a positive, uplifting mental image! And that image will take form.

What does imagination mean to you? Webster gives three definitions or usages of the word:

1. The act or power of forming mental images of what is not actually present.

2. The act or power of creating mental images of what has never been actually experienced, or of creating new images by combining previous experiences.

3. A foolish notion.

A majority of people seem to think of imagination only as described in the third usage: a foolish notion. "You are imagining things," we may say, implying that someone has an incorrect and foolish notion about something. If our children report that they are playing cowboys and Indians, and the Indians have their fort surrounded so they need more jelly sandwiches for the beleaguered cowboys, we may say, "What an imagination!" The inflection of our voice implies that such imaginings are more foolish than they are practical or constructive. And so the children may grow up to think of imagination as childish and unrealistic.

But we must remember that you and I were once children. When we learn the power of the imagination to form not only character but actual outer conditions, we will be more respectful of our children's imaginary games. Observing them in their imaginary situations, we will know that we are receiving a clear picture of the way they may react to situations when they are adults. Their subconscious minds aren't aware that this is an imaginary game; they are taking these experiences in as real experiences, and the mental reaction patterns exhibited in the imaginary games may be the basis from which they will react to actual life experiences. What a marvelous opportunity for the parent who is a Truth student to become as a little child and get into the game and influence the children to imagine acting in a Truth-directed way!

The first thing we want to tell ourselves is that imagination is *not* a foolish notion. Possibly it can be described in that sense in some instances, but we are wasting a tremendous source of power for changing outer circumstances if we lump all phases of the imagination under the foolish-notion category.

When you link the definitions given for the word *imagination* with the accepted mental law or principle that the subconscious mind cannot differentiate between a real and a vividly imagined experience, you have the clue to the condition-changing power of the imagination. For instance, the first definition is: *the act or power of forming mental images of what is not actually present.* This means that if you are meeting a health challenge, you can imagine yourself as you looked and felt when you were radiantly healthy. A spiritually scientific health therapy would be to sit back, relax, and vividly recall or imagine how you felt and looked and acted sometime in the past when you were expressing radiant health. The more vivid you can make this mental picture, the more your subconscious mind accepts it as actually happening, and it begins to picture forth that health.

Remember the second definition: *the act or power of creating mental images of what has never been actually experienced, or of creating new images by combining previous experiences.* Suppose you are a wallflower type of person. You feel uncomfortable at dances or public gatherings; this type of experience makes you cringe. Therefore, in your spiritual therapy for self-confidence and popularity, your imagination can create a mental image or picture of something that you may never have experienced—a mental image of yourself as poised, confident, conversing with ease, being favorably noticed and well-treated at a party or public gathering. Again, the more vividly you can imagine this, the more your subconscious mind accepts it as actually happening, and in the future real experiences will tend to cause you to react in this desired way.

You can see that the application of imagination

99

is unlimited in scope.

Salesmen can increase their number of successful closings.

Homemakers can furnish their homes with harmonious and comfortable furniture, and create an atmosphere of love, order, harmony, and gaiety.

An individual can work toward overcoming unwanted habits such as flying off the handle, selfishness, jealousy—even smoking or excessive drinking or eating.

Through the planned use of your creative power of imagination, you can develop poise, self-mastery, a success consciousness, a prosperity consciousness. You need only to remember and practice the principle that mental images, or the mental pictures you visualize on the screen of your mind through your faculty of imagination, have an inborn power to reproduce themselves. And the more vivid you make a mental picture, the more often you take time to hold this picture in mind, the more deeply it is impressed in the subconscious mind, and the more quickly it springs forth into actuality.

Someone may ask, "What has this to do with religion or with spirituality? Isn't that psychology?" Well, psychology is actually a department of religion, or the spiritual area of life! Long before the science of psychology was born, religion was working in the area of the mind. The Bible says: *For as he* (man) *thinketh in his heart, so* is *he.* (Prov. 23:7 A.V.) Psychologists centuries later say that "we react to our environment according to mental patterns in our subconscious minds and thus determine our future environmental conditions." What the Bible calls the heart, psychology calls the subconscious mind. Both are saying the same thing basically, but the Bible said it first. The familiar Golden Rule at first thought might seem more like an outer action than a mental principle—but remember, every outer action has to be preceded by a mental action. So again, this is primarily a mental teaching. The Golden Rule is actually saying, "Take time to imagine how you would like to be treated if you were in the other fellow's place; then act according to that understanding."

This teaching is effective and practical as well as inspiring because it takes the remarkable discoveries about the functioning of the mind and adds to them the concept of man as a spiritual being—one with (and a point of expression of) the one universal Spirit of God. In other words, we see that the mind is an instrument that the spiritual entity which you are uses to express the inner spiritual potentialities. Since your mind is such a wonderful instrument, the more you can learn about how it functions and the laws that govern its use, the better you will be able to use it to let God express your spiritual potential of health, harmony, successful accomplishment, and all the other things that are part of the abundant life that Jesus promised.

Imagination is a faculty that is capable of impressing your subconscious. So it makes good common sense to eliminate limiting and undesirable patterns from your subconscious (or heart) and to build new, perfect patterns.

Your mental pictures are not just harmless, ethereal little daydreams. Neither are they harmless "escapes from reality"; for those imaginings, those mental pictures, have what we might call a time bomb in them that will cause them to explode into an outer reproduction of themselves when they become charged enough through repetition.

You have shaped and molded your present life largely through your unwitting use of your faculty of imagination. Fortunately, you can reshape it and remold it through your new knowledge of its constructive use. The next time you look at yourself in a mirror, look past the reflected image. What do you see? Do you see a fear-ridden, worry-burdened, hopeless, cornered worm of the dust? Or can you see yourself as a child of God, bursting with potential power to meet and overcome any challenge that comes your way, with God's help?

If you need some help in forming your new image, open your Bible to the very first chapter and read: *Then God said, "Let us make man in our image, after our likeness; and let them have dominion . . . . " So God created man in his own image, in the image of God he created him . . . .* (Gen. 1:26, 27)

Where Did Those Limiting Thoughts Come From?

The cause of your limiting thoughts and feelings is a deeply ingrained predisposition to believe what people tell you (parents, teachers, authority figures, statistics, radio, television, newspapers, books, and so forth). Limiting mental images result when you believe that what has been done in the past is the limit of what can be done in the future, or when you believe that people and conditions have power to hurt or defeat you. In short, such limited thoughts can cause you to feel utterly dependent on the outer world, and to worship it fearfully as "real" and ultimately powerful.

Conquer your predisposition to worship the environmental world. Live from the premise that the spiritual universe is *real,* that it has irresistible power, and that it is friendly to you. Make God your only Source of energy, and let His infinite wisdom determine the channels through which your every need is fulfilled.

Exercise

Cross the threshold of meditation into the inner space of mind by closing your eyes, shutting the door on the chatter of outer activity, and relaxing.

Contemplate the unchanging "I" of you. Think: "My thoughts change and run like a stream, yet 'I,' the observer, remain. Desires and emotional states come and go, but my sense of 'I' endures unchanged."

Now think of this sense of "I," the real, eternal you, as translucent, a lens. And quietly, patiently wait for the light of Truth to shine through it from the spiritual universe. The Lord will be your ever-lasting light. Rest in that light.

Feel as if you are turning the focus of your faith from the outer world to the inner realm of reality; to the inner kingdom of God, as Jesus put it. Affirm: *I let go of limiting thoughts and feelings. I am receptive and responsive to the guidance of Christ, and a positive mental image of myself and my life is now being formed. I am grateful!*

The human body, scientists tell us, is composed of atoms; at the center of each tiny atom is a nucleus of light, energy, and intelligence. The thoughts that your central "I" identifies itself with stamp their character on the responsive garment of atoms. Let the healing, restorative light of the Christ dissolve firmly entrenched beliefs in limited vitality, or the inevitable destructive effects of time, by affirming: *I am free from limiting thoughts about my body. I form a new, positive mental image of my body; I am vitalized and renewed through Christ in me, and I am grateful!*

Because Solomon sought wisdom and understanding from the indwelling Lord, he: . . . *excelled all the kings of the earth in riches and in wisdom.* (II Chron. 9:22) Let your desire be for wisdom and understanding *and all these things shall be yours as well.* Know for yourself: *I am not bound by old thoughts and old conditions. I form a new, positive image about my life and affairs, and my life is changed and prospered through Christ in me. I am grateful!*

And lovingly know for others: *I see you receptive and responsive to the Christ within. You form a new, positive mental image; you are changed, your life is changed, and all is well.*

Benediction Thought

I move out from this brief moment of meditation with a new resolve to check my compulsive belief in and fear of outer conditions. I weigh their seeming power against God's power, and I smile. I form a new, positive mental image, and I am grateful!

VII

Nothing Is Impossible

During the first moon landing, one of the astronauts suggested that everyone pause for a few moments and think about the events of the last few hours and give thanks. During those brief moments of meditation, a stimulating and thought-provoking idea came to me: this space experience (including Neil Armstrong's first step on the surface of the moon) is a tremendously helpful analogy in understanding the role that Jesus played in revealing the infinite spiritual potentialities in man.

As soon as the first man placed his foot on the moon, in a very real sense he did it for each of us. With that one step, he broke through the veil of impossibility, doubt, and skepticism.

Something infinitely greater than the moon landing happened some two thousand years ago.

A man by the name of Jesus, from the town of Nazareth, had a dream, you might say. He taught that every individual is a child of God. Because we are children of God, we have access to the superhuman wisdom and power of our divine Parent—God.

For example, Matthew reports that Jesus taught: *"For truly, I say to you, if you have faith as a grain of mustard seed, you will say to this mountain, 'Move from here to there,' and it will move; and nothing will be impossible to you."* (Matt. 17:20) Then Jesus proceeded to demonstrate this truth. He changed water into wine; He fed thousands with a picnic lunch; He healed hopeless cases of illness; He raised the dead; and lastly, He broke through the veil of doubt and skepticism that man could ever overcome death. Jesus stepped through the experience of death and took that first step on the other side of death, proving that on the other side of death is *life!* Jesus demonstrated the tremendous spiritual potentialities within man. Now He turns to us, to you and to me, and says: *" . . . he who believes in me will also do the works that I do; and greater works than these will he do . . . . "* (John 14:12) And He says: *"Follow me."* (John 1:43)

But what has happened? Well, I guess the same thing has happened that would happen if we should put aside all our knowledge and experiments with space travel. In five hundred or a thousand years, the knowledge might be stored in dusty vaults. People a thousand years from now would develop the limited belief once more that putting a man on the moon was impossible, ridiculous, imaginative fiction. The events we have witnessed would be considered myth, or just something that gullible people believed—a miracle that is hard to swallow.

Of course, this can never happen, because hundreds of millions saw and were involved in all the moon landings. But the breakthrough, the first step into the kingdom of God in inner space that Jesus made, was witnessed by and involved only a handful of people. They tried their best to inform the world of what one man had done, and how because He did it, it was potentially possible for anyone and everyone to do it; but often they were not believed.

After a hundred years or so, the religion *of* Jesus became a religion *about* Jesus, even though He plainly taught that the same Father and the same power that indwelled Him and enabled Him to do what He did is the Father of every person and will enable anyone to do the seemingly impossible. Most people didn't really believe this, and remained content to build statues of Jesus and to think of Him as having a special dispensation from God. This happened in spite of His teachings that we all have the same Father He had, therefore we are all children of God, spiritual beings with the infinite potentialities of Spirit at our command.

We do not need to emphasize the traditions and creeds and theology that have accumulated through the centuries *about* Jesus and what He said. Rather, we need to build from the foundation that what Jesus taught is literally true. You *are* a child of God; God is your Father. God is Spirit, so as a child of a spiritual Being, you are a spiritual being. As a spiritual being, you have potentialities that far surpass and outstrip your human abilities. We must hold to the belief that what Jesus said about our being able to do the things that He did and greater things as well is literally true, and not just a grandiose but impossible promise.

Theory is fine and talk is easy; but how do we demonstrate this theory in our everyday living? There are three steps in releasing the spiritual energy within. We can become attuned to the wisdom of the divine guidance system in us and be lifted into orbit on our way to the accomplishment of what we may have thought was impossible.

These steps are *belief, persistent effort,* and *in-*

creasing knowledge of the application of spiritual principles. These three steps took us to the moon, didn't they? First there was tremendous *belief* in the minds of only a few people: Goddard, von Braun, and others. Gradually, more and more people became impassioned with and believed deeply in the possibility of a successful space flight, with the moon as their goal. *Persistent effort* was the next step. Goddard worked and worked. He took failures in stride and kept on working. At Cape Kennedy, the scientists continued to work while most of us who watched the final success were unaware of the perpetual activity there. *Increasing knowledge of universal principles* also played a part. The space scientists and technicians kept experimenting, studying, and sharing information. When they first started the project, some of the principles and methods used to land on the moon had not yet been discovered. But this didn't delay or discourage them. They kept working, and the new methods were discovered as they needed them.

Let us relate these three steps to the conquest of inner space and the mastery it will and does give to us.

Belief

What is it that seems so impossible to you? What in your life seems just as impossible to you as a moon landing seemed to people fifty years ago? Whatever it is, you have to believe with all your heart that it *is* possible—no matter how impossible it may look to human sense, to the masses of people. You have to desire it deeply in the belief that it is somehow possible!

Persistent Effort

If you are ill and your "impossible dream" is to be well and whole, you have to work consistently and persistently at affirming statements of health in your meditation times, such statements as: *My health comes from God. My body responds to the quickening of God's healing life within me. I am grateful!* Affirm statements like these not just once or twice, or once in a while, but faithfully, consistently. If your "impossible dream" is to get out of a life of poverty or lack or failure, consistently program into your dynamic subconscious mind a belief such as this: *The all-knowing Mind of Christ is in me. I think clearly; I know intuitively; and I act wisely, calmly, and confidently. My good flows to me from every direction, and I am open and receptive to it. I am grateful!* Yes, it's work, and there are periods when there is little evidence of outer results. This happened in the space program, too. But the scientists and engineers knew they were working with principles, and you know you are working with spiritual principles.

Increasing Knowledge of Spiritual Principles

Much of this comes automatically as you keep up your spiritual work. You grow spiritually; you grow in spiritual understanding. New ways and methods of realizing your oneness with God, the one Power and Presence in the universe, are revealed to you. But new and increasing knowledge of spiritual principles also comes through listening to Truth lessons, through reading the Bible, through studying books that teach spiritual principles, and of course, through faithfully practicing the Truth you presently understand in the everyday experiences of your life.

As you do this, even if it seems that nothing in the outer is changing, *you* are changing. And you *can* change if you will repeat to yourself the following spiritual logic—think about it, see if you can agree with it, see if you can totally accept it:

Jesus taught that God is our Father.

If God is our Father, then we are God's children.

Jesus taught that God is Spirit.

If our Father is Spirit, then as His children, we are spiritual beings.

If we are spiritual beings, then we have spiritual powers, capacities, and potentialities that go beyond our human abilities.

We follow Jesus in breaking through to the power of the kingdom of God within as we affirm and reaffirm in meditation:

I am more than human; there is that in me which is divine, for I am a child of a spiritual Father!

If you accept this as true, act from that premise. As you go about your duties of the moment, feel that you are being guided from the spiritual depths of your being. Especially when things seem to become confused or difficult, say to yourself, "It is time to switch over to IGS (Inner Guidance System)!" The "lift off" may seem to be slow, but be patient. Soon you will see the world, your world, from a new and higher point of view. Like our pioneering astronauts peering from their portholes at the Earth, you will say, "It's beautiful!"

Remember always that you are a child of God, and that with God's help nothing is impossible to you. You can learn how to face in a spiritual way problems that seem impossible to solve. If you have such a problem in your life, listen to the advice that the Bible gives you through a story of a battle that was miraculously won by the Israelites almost three thousand years ago.

These people, too, were up against superior and overwhelming odds. They were frightened in their helplessness; they were sure that defeat and disaster were in store for them. The story of this "mission impossible" is found in II Chronicles, the twentieth chapter.

The people of Judah were about to be attacked by three powerful armies—the men of Ammon, the men of Moab, and the men of Mount Seir. Jehoshaphat, the king of Judah, went to the house of the Lord and prayed aloud: "We are powerless against this great multitude that is coming against us. We do not know what to do, but our eyes are on thee."

Some time after Jehoshaphat's prayer, the people of Judah were assembled in the square; a prophet felt the spirit of the Lord upon him, and he stood up and proclaimed: " . . . *Thus says the Lord to you, 'Fear not, and be not dismayed at this great multitude; for the battle is not yours but God's.' "* (II Chron. 20:15) He continued: *"You will not need to fight in this battle; take your position, stand still, and see the victory of the Lord on your behalf . . . . Fear not, and be not dis-*

mayed; tomorrow go out against them, and the Lord will be with you." (II Chron. 20:17)

What is the spiritual principle here? Jehoshaphat was the king. A king in a Bible story can be said to represent the faculty of will. Jehoshaphat's going to the house of the Lord signifies that you must *will* to go apart, to turn within in meditation. In other words, you must say or think to yourself, "I will find some quiet place and pray about this problem." Your will is the executive faculty of the mind. It determines the direction you are going to move; whether you go to the right or to the left, whether you sit down or stand, the will must come first. You always say to yourself, or think to yourself, "I will sit down," or, "I will continue to stand." The will enters into every thought, every action.

Now that you have willed to have a quiet time of prayer and to take your problem to God within, and have affirmed that you will look to God for guidance and help, go about doing what is at hand to do, and at some time a *prophet* will arise among your "thought-people." That is to say, a strong thought will come to you or arise into your field of consciousness. A prophet always represents an intuitive feeling that suddenly comes to mind. It will say in one way or another, "Don't be afraid of this seemingly impossible problem! It is going to be solved in a perfect way, a way that is beyond your human ability."

As you listen to this inner voice, or feeling, or prophet, it will give you guidance. Perhaps you think of guidance as definite instructions about what to do next, and what to do after that, and so on. An important thing to know about inner guidance is that it deals with attitudes of mind that you should adopt, rather than with specific actions. The guidance for specific action will come when it is time to take the action, and many times even then you will take the right action without being aware of it at the time.

Let's examine the guidance given the people of Judah by the prophet in the Bible story.

First, *take your position*. What does taking a position mean? We say a legislator "took a certain position" on a controversial question; we mean that he made a choice. He was either for it or against it. The lesson for us is to take a definite position that we are going to trust God.

Second, *stand still*. This means that we must be unmoved in our faith that God is working with us and for us. Remember the story of the widow and the judge in the Bible? The widow "took her position and stood still." She wasn't about to be moved until the judge granted her request. Even so, we must not be moved from our faith that the problem will be worked out successfully in a divine way.

Third, our guidance will come, as we have said, not so much in *what* to do, but rather in the *attitude* we should have. Our inner prophet says: " . . . *Fear not, and be not dismayed; tomorrow go out against them, and the Lord will be with you.*" In other words, we should go ahead and do whatever is next to do. We are not afraid or dismayed. It isn't ours to know just what is going to happen until the time comes. But this whole situation is in the hands of a higher power, and it will work out in divine order and under divine timing.

To get back to the Bible story: The following morning, Jehoshaphat (who symbolizes the will) said to the people: . . . *"Hear me . . . Believe in the Lord your God, and you will be established; believe his prophets, and you will succeed."* (II Chron. 20:20) And then he appointed those who were to sing to the Lord and praise Him as they went out to battle, singing: " . . . *Give thanks to the Lord, for his steadfast love endures for ever.*" (II Chron. 20:21)

The lesson here is that our will must be firmly directed toward trusting God and believing that inner feeling or prophet which tells us that God will work all things in a perfect way. Also, we need to praise God and give thanks, even before the victory is won, or before the answer is apparent.

The three armies of Ammon, Moab, and Mount Seir began to fight among themselves because of some misunderstanding. So many of their number were killed in this quarrel and so weakened were their forces that the remaining soldiers of the opposition retreated from the field. The people of Judah had only to go down to the battleground and carry away the cattle, goods, clothing, and precious things. In fact, the Bible says that it took them three days just to carry away all the spoils!

What can we learn from this? Some may say that they were just lucky, that it couldn't happen again in a hundred years. Perhaps not, but it *did* happen when it was necessary that it happen! So many times the miracle answer to our desperate need seems to happen by "chance." When we tell a skeptic about it, he may say: "I don't see where God came in. You were just lucky. If this or that hadn't happened, you would never have had your perfect answer." Yes, but this or that *did* happen!

You see, we have to get over the notion that the activity of God has to take place in some spectacular way, with blinding flashes of light or thunderclaps. God works through the ordinary events and circumstances of life. There is no such

119

thing as "chance," for what we call chance is the working of law, or the result of failing to work with law.

The Bible has given us this story of a battle that was won without the lifting of a finger on the part of the victors—merely the lifting of voices in songs of praise and gratitude, and the lifting of consciousness to a place of steadfast faith in God. The spiritual teaching behind this story is that there is no impossible situation, no incurable disease, no unsolvable problem when we work with the Power to whom all things are possible.

Here are the important points to remember:

1. Your faculty of *will* is the executive power, the king of your thought people. Will to have a quiet time of prayer in which you give your problem to God, admit your human inadequacy, and agree to look to God for guidance.

2. At the right time, a *prophet* will arise as a definite intuitive thought or feeling within you. The inner prophet will give you assurance that God is with you, and will give you guidance by indicating what attitude you must take toward the facts as they present themselves.

3. Keep your thoughts filled with *praise to God*, and most important, be thankful that things will work out in a perfect way.

The rest is up to God. Things will happen; the

impossible will be accomplished! The *three days of gathering the spoils* represent the unexpected, unlooked-for blessings that will come out of your spiritual stand and spiritual victory.

A Triumphant Spirit

There is a triumphant Spirit in you that knows what to do in every situation! There is a triumphant Spirit in you that inspires you to purposeful, victorious living! There is a triumphant Spirit in you that heals and renews you! There is a triumphant Spirit in you that lifts you out of lack and assures you of supply for every need! What is this triumphant Spirit? It is the Spirit of God, the Spirit of truth, the Spirit of Christ, your innate divinity as a child of God and a spiritual being.

You can believe it or not; it is still there. You can call on it or not; it is still there. It is worth looking into; it is worth investigating; it is worth accepting as a premise. Accept it, and see what happens!

Exercise

Become still; withdraw inwardly for a time from the outer world that is constantly bombarding you with its sensory stimuli of sounds, scenes, duties, schedules. Just rest in the silence for a while. Enjoy the silence; let its peace settle into the far corners of your mind and into the very fibers of your body.

Now whisper softly: *There is a triumphant Spirit in me — a Spirit that knows what to do in every situation.* Get the feeling that although you know there are and always will be decisions for you to make, situations to face, challenges to overcome, somehow you will know what to do in every situation.

Now whisper again: *There is a triumphant Spirit in me that heals and renews me.* Vividly realize that your life flows from a Source deep within you, a Source that will ever sustain and vitalize you.

Visualize a huge storehouse filled with row upon row of boxes and cartons. Let this symbolize the storehouse of God substance everywhere present, ever available, undepletable.

Listen! A triumphant voice from within you is saying that God loves you and is looking after your every need, and your soul responds: *There is a triumphant Spirit in me that lifts me out of lack and assures me of supply for every need.*

Although your feet are set upon the path of Truth, like all Truth seekers you may feel an inner impatience, a hunger, a deep desire for greater understanding. Let the voice of God again assure you that you are making progress and that all is in divine order and under divine timing, as you whisper: *There is a triumphant Spirit in me that inspires me to purposeful, victorious living.*

Now you can feel your soul expanding to include and embrace every soul in the universe as you joyously speak these words of Truth for others: *There is a victorious Spirit in you that is ever inspiring you to the orderly unfoldment of your innate potential!*

Benediction Thought

Just as spring unfolds and bursts forth through blossom and bud, I let myself be constantly reminded of the same triumphant Spirit in me, ever inclining me, nudging me, pressing from within me to burst out of the tomb of self-preoccupation and into the sunlight of love and obedience to the indwelling Christ. I am grateful!

VIII

The Answer Attitude

There must be an easier way of living life than most of us are taking! It seems inconceivable that it could be the intent of universal Intelligence, which created this vast and wonderful universe, for man, His highest creation, to be the hurried, worried, tense, fearful, seemingly defenseless creature that most of us seem to be. Somehow we have made a mistake; somehow we have missed the message.

We need to discover that it is through the right use of the mind, our thinking faculty, that we can find the way of living that will make us masters instead of slaves, that will bring us inner calmness and patience instead of screaming tension and chronic anxiety.

Somehow, deep inside, we recognize that the answer is within us. But being so outer-oriented, we have come to believe that the answer lies in accumulating information, which we call knowledge. And so we worship the god of knowledge, not realizing that it is an impressive looking papier-mâché god that is merely stuffed with a lot of information. A computer serves the same purpose. Yet we continue to worship academic intelligence because we feel that if a person is academically intelligent, he must also be wise and happy, secure and trouble-free.

We send our children to college only partly because we feel a degree may assure them of higher paying jobs; we send them to college primarily because we want our children to be "smart," to learn something that will keep them from making the foolish mistakes we made. We may make fun of the "eggheads"—the intellectuals—but secretly we respect or envy them because we feel they *know* more than we do; and we erroneously equate this kind of knowledge with happiness, inner security, and the ability to make right decisions.

This, of course, is where we make our mistake. There is a world of difference between intellectual knowledge, or accumulated information, and true wisdom. The Bible is packed with promises that God will make us healthy, wealthy, happy, and peaceful in mind and heart; but nowhere does it say that an intellectual knowledge of mathematics, biology, history, literature, or chemistry is necessary to true happiness. Instead the Bible says: . . . *get wisdom* . . . *get understanding* . . . . (Prov. 16:16)

This is not to denigrate the accumulation of information through years of classroom lectures followed by experiment and observation. Intellectual knowledge has given us finely engineered cars, television, atomic power, and has enabled us to send men to the moon, and to accomplish many good things. But intellectual knowledge is obviously not helping us to live more happily, more serenely with more inward security.

The logical answer, it seems to me, is to get back to our starting point—mind—and reassess the situation. The Bible, which has been a great source of inspiration to people for centuries, talks about a sphere of intelligence called the kingdom of God that is located within us. It plainly implies that this inner source of wisdom and intelligence far transcends the intellect.

There must be, then, two directions in which the mind can face and work. One is the outer, where it can collect facts and information, observe results, and thus make the outer world more comfortable and safe. Yet there is also an inner direction, the exploration and right use of which will make our inner world (the more meaningful world) more comfortable, secure, and fulfilling.

Such logic is a good start, but it is only a start. We are so completely programmed with intellect-worship that when we try to explore the inner direction, the spiritual direction, we take with us all of our intellectual standards and tools. In Paul's first letter to the Corinthians, he writes: *The unspiritual man does not receive the gifts of the Spirit of God, for they are folly to him, and he is not able to understand them because they are spiritually discerned.* (I Cor. 2:14) In other words, when you seek to contact God—the kingdom of God, the sphere of infinite intelligence—for guidance, that guidance doesn't always come in ways that the intellect recognizes. So we may be skeptical about acting. Indeed, we sometimes think we have received no guidance at all, just because the intellect can't see it.

The intellect demands that there be a logical, obvious (or at least discernible) reason for everything. It wants to know where everything fits into the ultimate picture. When this demand isn't met, the intellect doubts, discards, ridicules, and goes on its own way worrying, fearing, desperately looking to books or the opinions of others whom it considers intellectually superior.

However, in spiritually educating your mind, you must learn to walk through what we might call the "intellectual darkness" by the light of faith. You must take as your premise the idea that God *is*, that God's wisdom is accessible to you, and that through God's love, infinite wisdom is momently guiding you, inclining you, motivating you toward your higher good.

Incidentally, this premise principle is used by scientists in their successful search for greater information about and knowledge of outer laws. They begin with a premise that is unproven but which they agree seems logical or true, and then they build from there. In spiritual experimentation and discovery, we take God—infinite intelligence, the reality and accessibility of the kingdom of God—as our premise. The next step from this premise is accepting the fact that infinite intelligence is greater and more knowledgeable than the intellect. Therefore, if in seeking to contact and act on guidance from God, the results do not pass the tests of the intellect or do not make sense to the intellect, this is not a valid reason for giving up, or for concluding that we haven't reached God, or that there is no God!

Here is a suggestion for seeking spiritual guidance, based on the premise that God *is*, that God's wisdom is accessible to you, and that because God loves you, His wisdom is flowing to you, motivating you from within, guiding you when you make yourself receptive to it.

On a piece of paper, write these words: "Father God, I look to you for guidance in regard to _____." Then write out your problem, the circumstance that is giving you trouble, the thing you need help with, the challenge you need guidance or counsel about. Having written that out, follow it with words such as these: "I am grateful, Father God, for Your perfect answer. I now release the problem as a problem, and enter into an answer attitude, calmly and patiently observing the unfolding answer."

In this way, you are using your power of mind rightly to seek wisdom from an inner direction. This, you can plainly see, does not prohibit or prevent you from using your mind in the outer direction to gather facts and information also. In fact, infinite wisdom works through all things, including any outer facts and information that you may be led to discover, to bring about the right and perfect answer. The intellect then takes its rightful place as a tool, an instrument, a servant, rather than the domineering boss, the vain and haughty king.

There is a "problem consciousness" and an "answer consciousness." Most of us stay in the problem consciousness and wonder why we can't seem to get an answer. It is like making out deposit slips and then wondering why the bank teller always *asks* us for money but never *gives* us any. We have to fill out a withdrawal slip in order to receive money!

Even so, learn to contact "command headquarters," infinite wisdom, when you are confused or need guidance. Then relax; the initial, unexpected, or painful phase of the problem is over. Help is on the way!

It is time to stop your frantic running to and fro, searching for all the answers outside yourself. Get into the answer attitude! Then you will cease trying to explain and understand all things in an intellectual way, and you will begin to tune in to God's answers directly.

A newscaster has said, "If electricians spent as much time trying to explain electricity as theologians and ministers spend trying to explain God, we would still be using kerosene lamps!" Certainly, this is a provocative thought. The best electrical engineers aren't agreed on just *what* electricity is, but they are agreed that it is, and that it is a tremendous source of power that can be channeled in countless ways when man conforms to the laws of its expression. And so they spend their time experimenting and discovering new methods and techniques for more efficient channeling of the power of electricity for beneficial use.

By the same token, we may not be agreed on a definition or explanation of God—and we never will be, for God is beyond description or comprehension by the intellect. But most of us agree that *God is,* and that God is a mighty power that can be and desires to be channeled into the lives of His children as the perfect answer to their personal and specific needs.

Jesus was great not only because He was a fine orator; He is the Elder Brother of mankind because He was a *doer.* It was His works that proved the truth of His words! He fed multitudes, He changed water to wine, He healed diseases, He raised the dead, and He raised His own body from the experience of death. Perhaps we cannot yet do the things that He did, but we can go forth on the assumption that the power He tapped to accomplish these tremendous works can also be tapped by us to solve our own daily problems. Jesus said very plainly: " . . . *he who believes in me will also do the works that I do; and greater works than these will he do . . . . "* (John 14:12)

Here is another simple technique that can help you get into the answer attitude that Jesus was talking about. This technique is very simple, yet it can open the way in your consciousness for God's power to flow into your life to solve your problems in perfect ways. The technique is based on the problem-solving power of a *question,* because the first step in finding an answer is to ask the question that is in your mind, honestly and sincerely.

When some problem confronts you, sit down in a place where you can be alone for a while and pick up a pad and pencil. Now write these words: "My Problem." Then ask yourself the key question: "What, exactly, *is* my problem?"

Don't let your thoughts whirl around on all the details of the problem. Don't go off on an emotional binge, so to speak; but think about your problem with the idea that you are going to put it down on paper where you can look at it and analyze it. Think about it calmly and carefully so that you can write it out concisely, clearly, and as briefly as possible.

After you have done this, underneath whatever you have written, write the words, "God's Answer." Now, write out God's answer by merely looking for all the negative words or phrases in the first paragraph, the one labeled, "My Problem," and substituting positive words and phrases for them in "God's Answer."

Let me give you an example. Under "My Problem," you might write something like this: I am nervous and tense about the new work they have given me at the office. I am afraid I will not live up to their expectations and all I have worked for will be lost. But I desperately need the money to fulfill my obligations here at home.

Through honest questioning and analyzing of yourself, you have frankly stated or pinpointed your problem. Now write "God's Answer." The first thing you see in your problem are those negative words, "nervous and tense," so look for their opposites. Write a new positive statement, replacing the negative words and phrases with positive ones: I am serene and undisturbed about the new work they have given me at the office. The next negative words were, "I am afraid I will not live up to their expectations and all I have worked for will be lost." Let's turn them around, look for their positive opposites. Change the statement to: Because God and I are an unbeatable team, I am confident of more than living up to their expectations, and this will prove to be a stepping-stone to my increasing success!

Now let's tackle the last sentence of the problem ("But I desperately need the money to fulfill my obligations here at home"). This statement definitely denotes a fear consciousness, a lack consciousness, a belief that your prosperity is dependent on outer things, outer conditions, outer business cycles. Whether you accept it or not, you are being material-minded, not spiritual-minded, when you look to and depend on material things as the source of your supply instead of looking to and depending on God as the Source of your supply.

What is needed here is a good, strong statement of the truth about your money or your supply; the kind of statement God would make, for remember, *this is God's answer*! Try the statement: God is the source of my supply; all my needs and obligations are fulfilled easily and abundantly. I am grateful!

Here is the stated or written problem again: I am nervous and tense about the new work they have given me at the office. I am afraid I will not live up to their expectations, and all I have worked for will be lost. But I desperately need the money to fulfill my obligations here at home. This is a legitimate problem, but what is God's answer? Let's read what we have written as God's answer to the problem: I am serene and undisturbed about the new work they have given me at the office. Because God and I are an unbeatable team, I am confident of more than living up to their expectations, and this will prove to be a stepping-stone to my increasing success! God is the source of my supply; all my needs and obligations are fulfilled easily and abundantly. I am grateful!

There is God's answer, and there is *your*

answer! Whenever you become problem-conscious—that is, whenever you find yourself fretting and getting upset over the problem—turn to God's answer and read it over, repeat it, concentrate on it, make yourself one with it, or (to use the term I like to use for myself), "grind" it into your subconscious mind.

Will it work? It certainly will. You are dealing with law, not just with words. The law is: . . . *as he* (man) *thinketh in his heart* (or subconscious mind), *so is he.* (Prov. 23:7 A.V.) You are consciously, carefully changing your thought, your belief about the situation. As we have pointed out in previous chapters, your thoughts, your beliefs, are *causes*; outer conditions are *effects*. When you change a cause, you automatically start into motion forces that change the *effects*.

Again, let me point out that the whole secret of this technique for channeling the power of God into working out your particular personal problem is to break through all the useless and emotion-depleting stewing about the problem and ask yourself honestly, "What exactly *is* my problem?" Make yourself answer that question honestly. Make yourself put it down in black and white, no matter how negative or painful the words you may have to use to express the real problem. You will never be in a receptive position to find the answer until and unless you face the real problem squarely.

Now begin to see God's answer by taking each one of those negative and painful aspects of the problem, turning it around to its positive opposite, and inserting in some way your basic belief that God is a very real and present power that is aware of you as an individual, that loves you as an individual, and that wants to help you as an individual; for this is Truth. This is Truth the Bible teaches, the Truth Jesus taught, Truth that Christianity is all about!

Too many people think that prayer is some sort of magical way you get God to do something for you without any change in yourself, without any real effort on your part. I suppose that is why many people want a so-called spiritual person to pray *for* them. They feel this will in some way change the condition without the inconvenience of their comfortable and crystallized beliefs being disturbed. But this can't be done. Someone can pray *with* you, helping you to find strength and understanding; but ultimately the answer has to come through your own consciousness.

Here, once again, is the technique to get into the answer attitude, simply and briefly:

1. Pinpoint the problem.
2. Pick out the negative words and phrases.

3. Turn them around to their positive meanings.

4. Reinsert the positive words and phrases.

5. There you have God's answer.

6. Meditate on God's answer, repeat it, totally accept it, and it will take form in your life in wonderful ways!

I Depend on God's Answer

"I depend on God's answer"—these words will open a whole new way of life for you if you seek to understand them and apply that understanding in your life. When you awaken in the morning and the multitude of duties, details, and responsibilities seems to press upon you like a dam ready to burst, whisper into the inner recesses of your mind, "I depend on God's answer."

Immediately a weight is lifted; immediately a sense of the rightness of this decision fills you. Suddenly you seem to have more strength—the lethargy is gone, the procrastination has vanished.

Tiredness, lethargy, procrastination about problems are but symptoms of spiritual forgetfulness—the forgetfulness that causes you to forget God's love and wisdom by taking personal responsibility for everything in your life, instead of giving the ultimate responsibility over to God.

Depend on God for answers, and He will answer you in perfect ways!

Exercise

Become still, and visualize a castle on a hill. Now see yourself outside the walls, exposed to hostile neighbors who seek to harm you. You run to and fro, fighting off one foe only to face another. Finally you come to your senses and go through the gate, into the castle.

Inside the protection of the castle, you find an invisible but very loving Presence who shows you the many interesting rooms of the castle and also points out how the strong walls will keep out any enemies, assuring you that here there is nothing to fear.

The castle is your own inner self. The invisible, loving Presence is the light within, God within you, the indwelling Christ. The enemies in this imagined picture are merely the circumstances and influences in your world of effects that seem to be ever pressuring you, upsetting you, exciting you to respond in negative ways.

Let that Presence guide you through the rooms of your symbolic castle. Observe, watch, wait. Soon understanding will come, bringing with it new insight, new meaning, new strength.

Know for yourself: *I depend on God's answer.*

He leads me in right ways and establishes order in all that concerns me.

Slowly, imperceptibly at first, the light begins to dispel the darkness in your consciousness. The words of the prayer affirmation above cease to be merely words, but become charges of light that pierce the darkness with rays of Truth. Rest in the light.

In the throne room of your castle is a sparkling fountain of the water of eternal life. Take the cup. Dip into the fountain and drink of the healing waters of Truth. Affirm: *I depend on God's answer. My whole being is cleansed and healed.*

Your enemies of lack, fear, and greed are all outside the walls of your castle. In the golden hall of abundance, you know that God is the unfailing source of your supply. Affirm confidently: *I depend on God's answer. I hold to the idea that God's law of divine order is adjusting and prospering my affairs, and I am grateful.*

As you think of your friends and loved ones, include them in this meditation time as you know for them: *You depend on God's answer. God is in charge of your life and affairs. He leads you in right ways and establishes peace, harmony, and happiness for all.*

Benediction Thought

I go forth from this time of meditation with two thoughts uppermost in my mind:

1. God is in charge of my life.
2. I depend on God's answer.

I feel and I know that this is so, and I let fear and worry slip away from my thinking. I enter a new, anxiety-free life of peace and accomplishment. I have an answer attitude, and I am grateful!

IX

A Technique for Self-Mastery

What is your spiritual center? It is the central "I" or I AM of your being. Say, "I AM" to yourself. Just as you have said "I" or "I AM," or thought it, so have thousands of other persons who have read this chapter or are reading it now. Each of them feels just as you feel—that sense of being alive, of being!

In other words, that basic "I" in you, in me, in every person, is the same. It is the spiritual center in each one of us. We are separate "I's," but each is an emanation from the one universal "I"—God.

Picture if you will a colander, such as is used in the kitchen to drain the water from noodles or vegetables. If you should pour a large pan of water into it, you would see a separate stream of water coming from each of the many tiny holes in the colander. This is a clear analogy of our relation to God and to all other individuals. The water represents the one universal Spirit of God, the one life force animating all things and persons. The holes represent you and me; they are outlets, channels, points of expression created for the specific purpose of allowing the water (the Spirit of God) to flow through, to find an outlet.

The water in any one of the streams is the same in quality as the water in all the others. Here we can see by analogy how the Spirit in each of us, or the spiritual center in each of us, is the same; and the Spirit in each of us is like the universal Spirit of God—it *is* the universal Spirit of God in individualized expression!

That is the nature of your spiritual center, the central "I" of you. It is Spirit, even as its source is Spirit. It is the same Spirit, in individualized expression, that is in every person. However, the important point we want to bring out is a fundamental principle that can be formulated as follows: We are dominated by everything with which our "I" becomes identified. And we can dominate and control everything from which we dissociate our "I." In this principle lies the secret of our bondage, and the secret of our freedom.

For instance, outer events of your day can cause you to react with a feeling of tension. Tension can be generated in your field of consciousness by various things: You may have an important meeting with a new client; you may have lots of grocery shopping to do; the phone may be kept ringing by talkative friends; the children may be cantankerous today; the house may look a mess—all sorts of outer things can generate a very real feeling of tension in you. But remember the principle: You are dominated by everything with which your "I" becomes identified. You can dominate and control everything from which you dissociate your "I."

When a feeling of tension is generated by these outer happenings and bursts into your field of consciousness, the usual reaction is to plunge your "I," your basic center of pure consciousness, right into this feeling. You may say, "I am tense. I am so tense that I feel like a tightly wound spring." Immediately the principle starts to work, just as the principle of gravity comes into operation the moment you drop an object.

The principle is that we are dominated by everything with which our "I" becomes identified. We have identified our self (or our I) with this feeling of tension in us, and we become dominated by it. It swirls our central "I" around in its clutches. In fact, we could liken these emotional feelings that arise within us, or that are generated within our field of consciousness as a result of outer circum-

stances, to emotional storms, like inner hurri-
canes. Our central "I," our basic self, our spiritual
center, is caught up in the emotional hurricane
and we are at its mercy. We are dominated by it
and feel that it is bigger and stronger than we are.

However, when we observe a hurricane on its
way, the wise thing to do about it is to get out of
the way of the storm, to avoid becoming enveloped in it. Or if we are too late and are caught in
the storm, the wisest thing to do is either to get
into a car and drive out of it, or find a place where
the storm can't get at us. In either case, what we
are essentially doing is separating ourselves from
the storm, dissociating, disengaging. We are free-
ing ourselves from being dominated by the storm.

So it is with an emotional storm of tension,
anger, depression, loneliness, jealousy, or discouragement. The moment we identify with it by
saying or inwardly acknowledging, "I am lonely,"
or "I am discouraged," we become caught up in
that destructive emotional force field, and become
slaves to it.

What we must learn to do is pause for just an in-
stant and look at it this way, "A feeling of tension
is trying to submerge me," or, "A wave of anger is
attempting to engulf me," or, "A mood of depression is seeking to pull me into its murky depths."
This, you see, changes the entire picture. Now

there are two forces defying each other. On one side is the strong and free "I," and on the other side is the wave or feeling or mood of tension, depression, or anger. We are aware of what is happening in us, yet we are not submerged in it, not dominated by it.

When you keep your "I" from submitting to or identifying itself with the emotional storm that seems very real within you, then you have two ways of dissipating it. As you stand away from it mentally, you can analyze it objectively. You can evaluate what will happen if it is allowed to continue. You can search for what caused this feeling of anger or discouragement. You will probably agree that most of the time the causes were rather silly. For instance, a destructive mood of irritation might have been caused by your childish reaction to the fact that no one rushed to answer the telephone and by the time someone finally got to it, it had stopped ringing. You have probably experienced many times when you were quite upset over something, and the next day or a week later you cooled down, so to speak, and felt a little silly trying to explain to someone why you were so upset. It usually seems trivial and unimportant. This is because the storm has passed; your "I" is no longer identified with it.

Another way of overcoming or dissipating an

emotional storm coming into your field of consciousness is to identify your central "I" with its source—God. As we have pointed out, your central "I" is Spirit—God's Spirit in you. You are ever connected to and one with God's own Spirit. However, when you identify yourself with a destructive mental attitude or emotional feeling, in effect you are causing a state of separation between yourself and God—a short circuit. Nothing seems to work out right when this happens, because you have cut off the power, or at least diminished it in your consciousness. You may get physically ill, you may feel you can't think clearly, you may also find that your intuition seems to be completely cut off, and you make many mistakes.

This principle of dissociating your "I" from a destructive emotional state and reattaching it to God's universal power is taught by Jesus through the prodigal son story. Leaving the Father's house and going into the far country is like letting our basic identity or "I" become identified with a destructive, negative, or limited emotional state such as hate, anger, resentment, inferiority, or discouragement. When we finally get tired of being kicked around—not by the world but by our own destructive mental and emotional reactions to the world—we find we can return to our Father's house. We can re-center, reidentify, our

"I" with its source—God.

We need to get back on the beam. Dissociate yourself from the emotional or mental state that is submerging your "I" and identify your "I" with God. Affirm, or command: *I am not discouraged. I am Spirit, and Spirit cannot be discouraged. I am one with God, and God is my strength!*

This is the path of spiritual mastery. This is the goal to strive for. The Bible teaches that . . . *he who rules his spirit* [is greater] *than he who takes a city.* (Prov. 16:32) To rule your own spirit means to place your I AM, your spiritual center, in control by refusing to allow it to become captured by transitory emotional states and compulsive habit-responses. Then you can turn control over to the guidance of the light of understanding within—God, the Father.

No matter what you have done or failed to do in the past, God loves you still. God has forgiven your mistakes—or sins, if you wish to call them that—for His unconditional love by its very nature implies and includes forgiveness. However, you may feel that past mistakes have left their mark on you, have changed you, altered you in a way that is working toward your detriment in the present and keeping you from attaining spiritual mastery. These "marks," these weaknesses, these false or limited beliefs, must be erased, eradicated, done away with in your consciousness.

The way to do this is to seek from this moment on to meet every outer experience from your spiritual center, instead of compulsively and helplessly responding from previously programmed mental and emotional patterns. In order to do this, you must first become vividly aware of your spiritual center. Through your increasing awareness of it, this spiritual center becomes stronger in you, more quickly and readily accessible to you.

Dig around in the multitude of thoughts and feelings that constantly churn around in your mind for that one permanent, unchanging factor—that basic core of your being that is fixed and constant. What is there about you that hasn't grown a day older or changed in any way for as long as you can remember? You are not the only person who is puzzled by the passing years. It is natural to feel that you are growing older, and yet strangely enough, you may also feel within yourself that you are the same person who stood on that high school stage to accept your diploma, or the same person who stood in front of a clergyman with one you loved and said, "I do." You don't really feel a day older in that sense.

The "I" of you has not changed or aged. Your body has changed, your attitudes about life have changed, your feelings about many people and things have changed. But there is one thing that hasn't changed one iota—the central "I" of you. This central "I" or I AM is your spiritual center. One of the essential characteristics of Spirit is that Spirit is unchanging. It never ages, never varies, is forever the same. And isn't this true of that central "I" of you?

Remember, it is through this spiritual center, the pure "I" of you, that you are connected to or one with God—the universal Source of power, wisdom, and life. It is through your central "I" that spiritual power and wisdom flow to you and through you. Your body, your intellect, your emotional nature, are not the real you—they are instruments and reflections of the true "I" of you.

Having found your spiritual center, the next thing you must learn to do is keep this spiritual center from being submerged in the various negative feelings, thoughts, and desires that may come into your field of consciousness. For when the "I" is submerged or taken captive by a transient feeling or mood, it is in a state of separation from its power source—God.

For instance, you may experience a feeling of tiredness or stiffness when you arise in the morning. But the "I" of you is not tired or stiff. The "I" of you is spiritual and is therefore incapable of being tired. Your body is tired and may feel a bit creaky—it needs a little stretching to limber up the muscles. So you say to yourself: "I will not submerge my 'I,' or my spiritual center, into this bodily feeling of tiredness. 'I' am not tired, only my body is. 'I' am spirit. Therefore, I will to do what is necessary to help my body get over its tiredness." Then you stretch as a cat does when it awakens, or exercise, or go ahead with your morning duties, knowing that the body will soon "snap out of it."

Practice doing this, not only with bodily conditions but also with mental or emotional conditions that you experience. Most of us have experienced the emotion or feeling of depression. You may say or think to yourself at such times, "I am depressed." There you go again, submerging the "I"—your spiritual center—into a passing emotional state, and thus weakening the reception of power from your spiritual Source! Remember that the "I" of you is not depressed, can never by the furthest stretch of the imagination be depressed, because the "I" of you is Spirit, eternally joyous.

What you really mean is that the "I" of you is beholding or is aware of a state of depression in you. The "I" of you then is free to make several choices. It can choose just to observe this emotional state of depression in you and its effects in your behavior and your life, simply waiting for the

150

depression to pass naturally. Or it can say: "I don't care to experience this feeling any longer. I will (to) take a walk and enjoy the beauty of nature; or I will (to) read a book, or play some favorite records; or I will (to) clean out a closet, or call on a customer." The choices for the "I" of you are un-limited. The trick is to get the "I" free from the emotional state of depression that seeks to capture it. You will find that when you dissociate your "I" from the emotional condition, power automatical-ly flows to you and you find yourself in command of the situation.

Listen to people talk, or listen to yourself talk, and you will see why so little God-power gets through into our lives. Our connecting source, our "I," seems to be constantly identified with and submerged in a torrent of negative, tension-producing, anxiety-ridden thoughts and feelings. A typical remark might go like this, "I am so tired today. My boss is on one of his efficiency kicks again. The air conditioner in the car went out and it will cost a hundred dollars to fix it. Every time I go to the supermarket, the prices on everything are higher. It is almost schooltime again, and the children don't have anything decent to wear— they've outgrown everything."

All day long, your spiritual center or your sense of "I" is completely captured and captivated, completely identified with a bodily feeling of tiredness, or anxiety about conditions at work, or tension concerning the air conditioner problem, or food and clothing prices. Feelings of resentment, impatience, fear, tension, or anger parade through your consciousness like a long funeral procession of cars, and your sense of "I" jumps into each one.

The point is, how in the world can your spiritual center, your "I" (which is the basic point of connection between you and God, the power and wisdom source), receive power, guidance, and understanding from the Fountainhead when it is constantly engaged in identifying itself with all these negative feelings?

Picture a switchboard operator who is just learning the job. Her teacher stands behind her, telling her what to do, but she doesn't hear the teacher because she is listening to or identifying herself with all the conversations on the various lines she plugs into. The board becomes completely jammed because in trying to give her attention to so many conversations, the operator impairs her ability to function skillfully. She becomes upset, weak, drained, filled with tension.

The light of understanding within you is the teacher; the switchboard is your mind. The calls and conversations are the constant barrage of challenges, outer happenings, responsibilities that are coming in through the lines of your five senses to your central "I," the operator. Each of the outer calls or happenings in your world of effects, your environmental world, carries with it an emotional charge. As you listen to or identify with the outer happenings, you are exposed to this emotional charge, and in time it weakens you, drains you, exhausts you. The solution is clear. First, take frequent times to get away from the switchboard entirely and listen to the Teacher; turn your full attention, in prayerful meditation, to the light of understanding within.

Second, when you do return to the switchboard—that is, when you enter again into contact with your outer environment with its many demands, challenges, and duties—do not let yourself become so completely involved in the incoming calls. In other words, control your reactions to the emotional charges in each incoming call. If you find yourself responding with emotion (anger, fear, resentment, impatience—you know the list), each incoming charge is tremendously increased, and it drains you. However, if you do not respond emotionally, if you retreat to your spiritual center for guidance as to how to respond, you find the incoming emotional charge is dissipating and disappearing. You thrive on your work, you thrive

153

on life; and when you love life, life loves you in return and contrives all sorts of good things for you, its lover.

As time goes on, each of your weaknesses, each of your past mistakes, will come into your life for rehandling. The reason for this is that until you pass a test in life, you are continually tested, continually given the opportunity to meet it successfully.

Already you are learning how to respond correctly to an outer challenge or temptation by refusing to respond emotionally. Instead, you are learning to retreat for a moment to that spiritual center within where you are motivated by the inner light to choose wisely, to act wisely, and thereby to erase the scars of previous mistakes or apparent failures. You are well on your way to true self-mastery!

Spiritual Self-Mastery

Jesus taught that each individual is one with God and has immediate access to God's presence and God's kingdom. Therefore, it is not necessary to go through any intermediary in order to contact God and to achieve true self-mastery.

Jesus spoke through the Christ self when He taught that anything you ask of the Christ self in *you* will be accomplished. "Open up in the name of the law!" means that the law is the authority for the command. When you ask for self-mastery, wisdom, wholeness, or supply in His name, you are saying that the Christ in you is the authority for your request. You are appealing to the Christ potential in you, and its authority is supreme. To ask in the name of Jesus Christ, then, is to ask through the authority of the universal I AM as individualized through you.

Exercise

Relax! Stop reading for a moment or two and close your eyes. Just heave a deep sigh and let your body and your thoughts settle down, the way a sheet settles down when you make the bed— slowly, gently, effortlessly.

Now listen to the sounds around you for a moment, and bless them. In this way, they become your friends, and they won't intrude on your attention as you meditate. Say to yourself, "I AM." Then say or think to yourself, "God is that universal sense of I AM which is individualized through every person as his personal sense of I AM. God is that universal sense of I AM which is individualized in and through me as my personal sense of I AM. Truly, God and I are one, and God is the One!"

155

Through the doorway of your I AM, you have entered into the kingdom, and you ponder Jesus' words: *"The kingdom of God is not coming with signs to be observed; nor will they say, 'Lo, here it is!' or 'There!' for behold, the kingdom of God is in the midst of you."* (Luke 17:20, 21)

The kingdom of God is a kingdom of light—not light that you can see, perhaps, but just as there are some light waves imperceptible to your physical eyes, so there is a spiritual light that is beyond any physical measurement. This light is perceived by your spiritual nature and is focalized and magnified by the faculty of faith. Affirm for yourself: *In the name of Jesus Christ, wisdom and divine guidance are mine. I act on my faith and I achieve self-mastery over my mind and affairs.* Now bask in that light.

The "I" of you is invulnerable to illness or deterioration. Identify its invulnerability with your physical garment of flesh as you affirm: *In the name of Jesus Christ, life and health are mine. I achieve self-mastery over my body and I am made whole!* Surrender to that healing light.

The kingdom of God contains the perfect fulfillment of everything you could possibly need for your comfort, happiness, and personal success. Give thanks as you affirm: *In the name of Jesus Christ, success is mine. I achieve self-mastery over my prosperity, and I joyously accept my good!*

Bless others as you know for them: *In the name of Jesus Christ, you are guided, strengthened, and prospered. You achieve self-mastery, and divine order and timing are established in your life and affairs.*

Benediction Thought

Through these moments of meditation, I am exposing my center of awareness and will to the motivation of God's Spirit within me. Thus, little by little I break my hypnotic attachment to the outer motivation of the world. As I achieve spiritual self-mastery, I live from the will and wisdom of God, and I am grateful!

X

How to Change Your Life

Sometime, someplace, each of us must come to a point where we say, "I've had enough of this kind of life. I want to change. There must be more to life than I am experiencing."

But where do we go to change our life? Where do we go to change our inner self? Do they offer such courses in universities, like the courses that are turning out engineers, physicists, specialists in every field? No, but we do possess a vast body of knowledge in our society. We can send a picture of something that is happening in London all the way to Los Angeles at the moment it happens, by bouncing some electrical vibrations off a piece of metal miles above the Earth. We can send men to the moon.

Yet the very men and women whose minds have been programmed with this fantastic knowledge are often groping around within themselves, saying, "There must be more to life than I am experiencing. Where is meaning for my life? Who am I? Why am I?"

If your security is no more than the knowledge that has been programmed into you through school, through your job, then if something happens so that your knowledge is no longer needed, what will you do?

A spiritual approach to life holds the only answer. In the world of effects, we may seem to be merely ants, computers, objects to be used. But in the inner world, the spiritual universe—or to use Jesus' words, the kingdom of God—we are individuals; we are points of expression of a miracle power. We have meaning and purpose because we are parts of a spiritual whole, and every part is important to the whole—just as the smallest part of your body is important to the normal and perfect functioning of the whole body.

When we seek knowledge and understanding of the spiritual universe with the same desire and drive that we have heretofore applied to seeking knowledge of the outer universe, we will come to know that the inner universe is our true security. We are not expendable in God's sight, in the way we may be to companies that use our intellectual knowledge or our physical muscles.

This inner security might sound impossible and totally unrealistic to the outer-oriented mind. And it *is* unrealistic if your definition of reality is the ever-changing outer world. But if you are truly fed up with a life that is premised on reality being this outer world, made up of clustered atoms formed into shapes of buildings, trees, sofas, and stoves, then you must be willing to change your premise!

Even a scientist changes his premise when the original one isn't working out, or when he feels that another premise might take him further. Einstein opened up a new frontier of knowledge because he discarded a previous premise and introduced a new one.

The premise that reality is universal power and presence, an originating intelligence, a creative First Cause that is summed up in the three-letter word *God*, is not a new premise. Mankind has a Book that has been preserved through the centuries which teaches, proclaims, announces, and reveals this premise. Millions of people revere the Bible. They are incensed if anyone misuses or speaks against it. The Bible is the best-seller of all time. Yet in reading it, often we do not understand it (or we do not want to understand it), for the Bible tells us to base our life, our thoughts, our responses or reactions to the world of form, on the premise that there is a universal and transcendent power and intelligence of which we are points of expression—or in simple language, whose spiritual children we are.

"Turn to God!" the Old Testament teaches us over and over again. " . . . *seek first his kingdom and his righteousness, and all these things shall be yours as well,"* (Matt. 6:33) the New Testament teaches. But we are so outer-oriented that when we read that we should turn to God, we tend to look for some outer thing to turn to instead. Throughout time, people have turned to temples, to images, to rituals. In trying to fit Jesus' teachings of God as invisible, everywhere-present Spirit into our outer-oriented mentality, we may have postulated a figure in the sky on a throne and turned to God by addressing the heavens.

Today we often are not certain where to turn. Many simply turn away, or turn off with the "God is dead" theory. Others turn to church organizations that tell them how to think and what to think, with the guarantee that salvation lies in strict obedience to organizational rules and dogma. Others try to substitute idealistic causes for God and speak in terms of total commitment, involvement, love for others. And yet the means by which they often seek to bring about these ideals may not be above hate, violence, anger, revenge, and disdain for those who do not agree with them.

161

Perhaps this is essentially all good, because by the process of elimination, at least, we are bound to come to the last resort—the hard-to-believe, so-close-that-we-can't-see-it, so-simple-that-it-can't-be-true conclusion that God is found right within us, and then we can turn to God by turning within our own being.

What if our universities would decide to teach courses from the Bible—a textbook that has outlived all their erudite, multi-syllable-worded textbooks? What if they accepted the premise of this textbook and researched the untapped and unexplored areas of prayer and meditation? What if we looked for new techniques of going within and charting the inner path that leads through our basic sense of identity—our I AM—to the kingdom of God that is the common source of all persons and things?

But we need not wait for the universities or for a great mass movement toward acceptance of an inner universe, a spiritual universe. You and I can begin today, right where we are, with the knowledge and understanding we presently have.

Take time to go apart and sit quietly alone. Get away from all the distractions that clutter your consciousness so that you cannot focus your attention on the inner universe; do not admit the distraction of television, newspapers, books (even

Truth books).

Then as you sit quietly in meditation, gently ease all distracting thoughts from your field of consciousness. Don't hurry them, don't force them to go; simply become aware of them, bless them, and invite them to go. This may take more than a couple of minutes, for your outer-oriented *ego* with its go-go need for continuous outer distractions may say, "Let's get it over with. Hurry up! You've been sitting here long enough. Let's do something useful!"

But if you are serious about changing your life and the direction in which you are headed, let something deeper than your personal ego take charge. This something cannot easily be described or labeled, but it can be experienced. We can call it the super-ego, the indwelling Christ, or the basic I AM of you. But whatever you call it, you can experience it as a feeling that is greater than the personal ego—something that sees through the personal *ego* and knows that without this spiritual essence we are helpless, simply thrashing our way through life.

Through this spiritual essence, we intuitively know that life was not meant to be miserable—it was meant to be exciting! There is something exciting about the very word *exciting*! Recall some exciting times, such as the day you were married, or those wonderful, exciting moments at the amusement park when you were a child, or the weekend you attended your first college football game. The word *exciting* seems to fit perfectly every memorably happy experience of your life.

If we look up the derivation of the word, seeking a clue to its magic, we find that it is a combination of the Latin word *citare*, meaning "to arouse," and the prefix *ex*, which means "out from." To be excited, then, is to be *aroused out from* a feeling or attitude of boredom or lethargy. Yet there is another usage of the word *exciting* given in the dictionary. This is also a commonly used word in the science of electronics. It means *to energize; to produce a magnetic field, as in energizing a dynamo.* The dictionary definition continues: *A dynamo may be excited by a separate machine, or by a portion of the electricity which it itself produces.*

I think we have here a clue to the secret of making your life exciting. After all, you are filled with power, spiritual power. As a child of God—or a point of expression of the one power and presence, God—you have much in common with a dynamo. The dictionary says a dynamo may be excited (energized) by a separate machine; or it may become self-exciting by utilizing a portion of the power inherent in it. I suggest that the reason most people find excitement or exciting experiences so few and far between is that they depend on being excited by "a separate machine," so to speak. That is, they depend on external events or people to excite or energize them—a football game, a camping trip, a movie, a friend. This all seems harmless enough, but the problem arises when we fall into the habit of looking for and depending on other people, events, or conditions for our excitement, our energy, or a feeling of being really alive.

Once we fall under the spell of this habit, we are hooked. We are too impatient to wait for something exciting to happen. By "something exciting," we mean something that will excite us, arouse us out of the painful boredom, emptiness, loneliness, lack of energy, lack of feeling that we are truly alive.

We may seek some outer stimulus that will do the trick. This could be drinking or experimenting with dangerous drugs; but if the monitor of conscience won't permit us to indulge in such outer excitements, we turn to long sessions of playing games of some kind, or even just complaining, finding fault.

Have you ever met people whose conversation is limited to criticizing the government, taxes, or politicians? These are good dodges for the energy-parched ego, because such people can appear righteous; they can wear the present-day halo of being "involved," while actually they are looking for excitement, for a sense of being alive, for an emotional "kick" from some outer source.

Although I am not an electronics engineer, I imagine that the sentence from the dictionary that reads: *A dynamo may be excited, by a separate machine,* implies that if that separate machine runs out of power, the dynamo runs down. And so it is with these "separate machines" or outer sources of stimuli that mankind looks to and depends on for excitement, for energy, for a feeling of being alive. They have a habit of running out of power, running out of excitement; then the individual who depended on them feels lost until he can find some other outer stimulus to excite him, to make him feel alive once again.

These outer stimuli tend to lose their power to excite us, and once again we feel we are out of energy. We become bored, lonely, and feel only half alive, and we may begin to complain more and more. Some people can go on for years and years complaining about everything under the sun and getting their excitement from this. But this is costly, because complaining, which necessarily involves resentment, anger, and hostility, places a terrific burden on the physical body.

There is a sense in which we can actually become in bondage to these outer sources of excitement. Just like the kind of electric dynamo that has to have a separate machine to energize it, so we may feel we have to have outer excitements such as drink, drugs, complaining, compulsive card playing, compulsive bowling or golf. We may tell ourselves that these are only relaxations; if this is true, then we need to try giving them up for several months, to see how we feel about this.

The answer to the problem as I see it is to work toward becoming the second kind of dynamo that the dictionary mentioned: a dynamo that *may be excited (energized) . . . by a portion of the electricity which it itself produces.* This means that it is not dependent on an outer source for energy. In making the analogy with ourselves, this means we are not dependent on other people, events, or conditions—on drink, drugs, games, or complaining—in order to feel alive, happy, and fulfilled.

The way to become excited or energized, or to feel fully and completely alive, is to look to and depend upon our inner contact with that inner energy field we call God, or the kingdom of God. This does not mean that we do not play golf, or bowl, or enjoy relaxation in many outer ways. We do not retreat from the world. However, the point is that we do not *need* these things in order to be happy. We are not slaves to outer things—we are free souls!

It may not be easy to break our attachment, our bondage, to the environmental world as the source of our excitement. The brainwashed ego may give all sorts of excuses and arguments. And even if we see the logic of turning within for the kind of excitement or energy that is lasting and satisfying, it may not be accomplished in the wink of an eye.

However, here are two suggestions for a start: first, make more than a halfhearted attempt to meditate; second, live deeply in the present moment. If you are going to work on the premise that real energy, real excitement (by which we mean that feeling of being fully and enthusiastically alive) comes from a source within you, then it follows that you have to spend some time getting acquainted, being at home in those far reaches of inner space.

Once you are launched on a program of inner-space exploration and discovery—once you taste, experience, make a part of yourself that inner atmosphere of peace and wonder and humility— you find a new quality in your consciousness. You find that you look forward to living deeply in the present moment. This happens not just in your meditation times but as you live the hours and

168

days of your entire life. You begin to see that eternal life is a question not of length but of depth. Eternal life reaches down deeply into the present moment, for the present moment of time is all there really is. The past is a memory stored in some cells in your brain; the future is as unreal as a dream. There will be a future, but when it gets here it will be *now*. And what it contains when it gets here is determined by your thoughts, attitudes, emotional states, in the *now*.

The one universal and inescapable law is the law of cause and effect. Where there is a cause, there must be an effect; where there is an effect, there must have been a cause. The present moment is filled, even cluttered, with effects; but it is also waiting to be impregnated with causes. You reap in the now, you sow in the now. Jesus said: *". . . the fields are already white for harvest,"* (John 4:35) even though He was looking at a freshly sown field.

You can live a continuously exciting, deeply fulfilling life, instead of being limited to the sporadic exciting days, so few that you treasure them as fond memories. Instead of getting caught up in the futile pursuit of outer excitements which can eventually enslave you and leave you sick and unhappy, you can become self-energized by the power of God from within you. Through medita-

169

tion, you find you can live a truly wonderful life in the present moment.

Gradually the light of the I AM suffuses your consciousness, spreading like the light of dawn, and you feel an inner peace and rightness. As you persistently keep these times of meditation, that inner light and peace and rightness becomes ingrained in you, becomes a part of you—in just the way that formerly every outer event you experienced became a part of you, every emotional reaction became a part of you, every satisfied desire (good or bad) became a part of you. Now you are working with something new, something strange and unfamiliar, perhaps, but something good, something spiritual, something real, in the sense that God is real.

Gradually you change. Your habits change, your friends sometimes change, your values change, your circumstances change, and your life changes. You are no longer utterly and hopelessly dependent on other people and outer conditions to make you feel right or good or secure. You are beginning to take the Bible seriously, and you find, in a new and wonderful way, that every one of its promises is true.

Your security is based on a new premise: God is a reality, and you are a child of God with the kingdom of God as your divine inheritance.

In the Peace of Prayer,
I Let God Change My Life

Peace is power, for out of stillness, strength is born, and out of inner harmony, productivity flourishes. Peace cannot be manufactured, or inherited, or won through outer victories. It is bestowed from within to the humble of heart who have learned to see the changing world of effects as superimposed over the unchanging, eternal goodness of God. Peace is an atmosphere of mind, drenching every thought, desire, and feeling. Its character is gentleness and softness, yet inflexible dependence on God alone.

You are a part of an invisible multitude; but even in the multitude, you do not lose your individuality, for each of us now follows his own path into the inner recesses, the private places of his own consciousness. So together, yet apart, we strengthen each other and encourage each other. Traveling together, yet alone, we see strange and wonderful insights which we may not be able to share at a verbal level, but that somehow we do share at a deeper level.

Your own feeling of inner peace and oneness with the Spirit that binds us all together gives you a clue to what others are experiencing, and you are glad—and that is love! Rest in that inner peace.

171

Exercise

Deep in that inner "well" of Self, remember that the only unchanging thing about you is your sense of "I," the I AM of your basic sense of being. Think of an electrical outlet in your home. You can attach a toaster cord to it, or a blender, or a lamp, or a radio . . . or you can disconnect. So it is with your basic sense of "I"—you are constantly attaching or dissociating thoughts, desires, or feelings to it.

Just as the electrical outlet is not the source of power but the focal point of its distribution, so is your "I" or I AM the distribution point for the power source—God. The thoughts, desires, and feelings to which you choose to attach your "I"— whether they are constructive or destructive—are empowered by the one Power. Therefore, choose well. Affirm: *I am one with the universal power source—God. Universal life energy is flowing to me and through me now, changing my life. I feel it!*

Receive the illuminating peace of God as you know for yourself: *The peace of God fills me now, changing my life. I am an open channel for the inflow of divine guidance.*

As you think of your mind and your physical body, know that you are divinely blessed and whole. Affirm: *The peace of God fills my mind and body. I am changed, renewed, relaxed, re-freshed, and healed!*

Fill your thoughts concerning your prosperity with the peace of God by using this statement: *The peace of God fills my mind, changing my life, and drawing to me the perfect fulfillment of my every need, and I am grateful!*

Surround others with these peaceful blessing thoughts, as you know for them: *The peace of God enfolds you, and your life is changed in wonderful ways!*

Benediction Thought

As I again turn to my outer environment and its many duties, I am continuously fed and empowered by God's peace, wisdom, and light. My life is blessed and changed, and I am grateful!

XI

Putting Truth into Practice

Are you in the midst of some problem that is bothering you, giving you sleepless nights, perhaps, or making your food taste flat, causing you to go around with a strained, tense, lost look and feeling? If you are, I want to give you two specific ideas that can help you to handle that problem spiritually, handle it easily, effortlessly, even joyously—and what is more important, successfully!

The first specific idea is: look at the date on your calendar. Then say or think to yourself, "Time does not stand still. The ever-present now constantly moves forward. This I acknowledge as an incontrovertible fact. Therefore, there will be a time a month, six months, or a year from now when I will be looking back at this present time and problem. The problem will, at that time, have been resolved somehow, and I will be able to see how all of these now perplexing and confusing facets of the problem worked out.

"At that time in the future, be it a month, six months, or a year from today, I will also be looking back at how I reacted to the problem. If I reacted with fear, if all my faith in God seemed to go out the window, if I felt inside like an emotionally immature child, if I cringed inside and tried to find ways of escape like alcohol, self-pity, or indignantly trying to blame other people, then no matter how the problem worked out, I will be ashamed of myself, disappointed in myself. Perhaps nobody else will know how badly I reacted mentally and emotionally to the problem, but I will know, and I have to live with myself.

"On the other hand, when that time in the future comes, be it a month, six months, or a year from today, how good it will be if I can look back on today's date and know in my heart that I handled the problem in a spiritual way. I will remember that I wrote out an affirmation and used it faithfully, repeating it even in my car on the way to work. I will remember how I *made* the time to have brief quiet times when I would meditate on the affirmation. I will remember how difficult it may have seemed to believe in such an intangible presence as that presence and power we call God, and how the overwhelming facts of the problem seemed so impossible to change. I will remember that I had the courage to push through my doubts and hang on to my faith in that invisible and intangible power."

Here you stand; that time in the future *will* come—a month, six months, or a year from today—and now is the time that you make your choice, your decision as to which of these two feelings you are going to experience a month, six months, or a year from now!

Are you going to be ashamed of the way you mentally reacted to this problem? Is it going to be a painful memory that you won't like to think about, because it will remind you of what a weak, ineffective, and immature person you seemed at the time (and, unless you change, still seem) to be? Or are you going to be proud of yourself that however the problem turned out, you handled it by really trying to use all the Truth you knew at the time?

Now is the time to make your choice. You can't turn back the clock a month, six months, or a year from now!

I have found in my own experience that this mental flight of imagination into the undeniable future is of tremendous help in enabling me to square my spiritual shoulders, so to speak, to shake off those "little foxes" of fear and doubt, and to get to work on finding an affirmation that suits the problem at hand. For example, I like to use an affirmation that plainly states that I am a spiritual being, a child of God, and that God's Spirit does indwell me and is giving me the courage and strength to do what needs to be done. The statement should include the thought that God's infinite wisdom is guiding me into right action, and that beyond what I do or say, there is an invisible intelligence that is working all things together for my highest good, and for the highest good of all concerned, in a perfect way and under perfect timing.

Then, regardless of *how* the problem works out, I find I am a happier and more secure person inwardly. I can assure you that if you use this method, the problem you may be facing will work out in a different and better way than it will if you choose the way of fear, resentment, anger, self-pity, or any of the other emotional responses that we like to excuse as "only human."

Certainly you are human; but you are not "*only* human." You are made in the image and after the likeness of God, as the Bible plainly states in the first chapter of Genesis. Although we believe in the Bible, we need to realize the far-reaching implications of what the Bible is actually saying. Then the "only human" excuse goes out the window, for we must face the fact that we are a combination of Spirit and flesh—or divinity expressing through humanity.

The second specific idea in approaching present problems concerns a definite technique for contacting the source of all wisdom and power. You need to get in tune with God, with the invisible Presence that *knows* how to work out your problems successfully.

There is really only one place to get in tune with God, and that is in your mind. You are "connected," so to speak, with God—not through your hands or your big toe, or even through any church organization. You are connected to God through one point only—your mind.

Therefore, the idea is to get a thought, a belief, in your mind that is consistent with what is true of God. For instance, is it true that God's Spirit indwells you and that God is all-wise? Is it true that anyone who has this tremendous power that we call God working with and for him has nothing whatsoever to fear, and that the outcome of any project that He and God tackle together is certain to be successful? If you believe that these things are true of God, then shape them into a statement of that Truth. For instance: *I totally accept the belief that God's Spirit indwells me and that infinite wisdom is guiding and strengthening me. I approach this so-called problem with the attitude that it is an opportunity to work with God, and to see at firsthand how this miracle-working power can straighten all things out and bring undreamed-of good out of seeming trouble. I am grateful!*

Of course, this statement is a little long; it is often better to use a shorter statement that you can remember and repeat often, during your active moments and during moments of meditation. But if you give careful thought to formulating a longer statement and then cut it down to a more concise form, you will find that all the ideas and thoughts you entertained while formulating the longer statement will automatically be packed into the shorter one as you repeat it. For instance, you might reduce the long statement given earlier in this way: *I totally accept the belief that I am one with infinite wisdom and that I am now being guided into right action. I have unwavering faith that God is bringing forth a unique and divinely perfect outworking of this challenge. I am grateful!*

Just repeating this once isn't going to get your mind in tune with God, because your mind has deeper levels than the conscious level. For your "whole" mind or being to be in tune with the "God vibration" in the universe, the subconscious mind must also accept and agree with this statement of Truth.

How do you get the subconscious level of mind to accept a statement of Truth you have formulated on the conscious level? This is done through a combination of depth meditation and repetition. Don't let the term *depth meditation* frighten you. I am merely using that term to differentiate from the usual type of prayer that most of us learned as children when we "talked" to a person called God whom we pictured with a long, flowing beard; we listed the people we wanted Him to bless, and requested good weather for our picnic or whatever.

You may call depth meditation "concentrated prayer," if you wish. It is that mental act of going down deep within yourself, leaving the surface distractions—the noises, the darting thoughts, the kaleidoscopic mental pictures of past events and future plans. Say to yourself, "I am going down deeper and deeper into the well of my inner, unchanging Self." Your inner well of Self opens into the allness of God. As you go further from the surface distractions, you begin to feel the pleasant atmosphere of peace, the understanding of oneness.

Now take your previously prepared statement of Truth. Repeat it slowly. Each word will seem to burst at the seams and spill out new understanding, new rightness. This should be done at least once a day, and more often if possible. In addition, place your written statement of Truth where you can see it often so that your *ever-alert* subconscious mind can feast on it and become deeply impressed with it.

Remember, there are two specific things that you can do: (1) Project yourself into the future in imagination, and look back at how you want to see yourself handling this problem. Know that if you want to look back and remember yourself as handling it in a spiritually adult and mature way, the time to decide that is *right now*. (2) Get out a paper and pencil and write out a statement of spiritual Truth about the situation; then shorten that statement into one you can remember and repeat. Work at it while you are about your active duties and also in frequent times of meditation—especially when fears or anxieties about the problem arise in your mind and heart.

We have all faced times when it seemed that we just couldn't go on, when life seemed to have us backed into a corner from which apparently there was no escape. We have gotten through these times somehow, but some of these experiences may have left scars in our minds, and subsequently in our lives. Now we know that we can meet these times of crisis more successfully than we may have done in the past.

Let's face it, life is made up of successive crises, some large, some comparatively small. But if we were to count the number of times we have said, "I just don't know what I am going to *do!*" or words to that effect, in the last few months, we would realize that it is high time we started to learn how to meet a crisis experience successfully.

Let's analyze a crisis. It has three stages, like a space rocket. The first stage is the sudden appearance of a problem-situation. The phone rings and we get distressing news, or a memo is sent around at work announcing a new company policy that may jeopardize our job, or some physical symptoms appear that we feel may be the forerunners of a serious health challenge.

In the first stage of a crisis, your world is jarred loose. The comfortable pattern of your daily living is disrupted and you feel bewildered, lost, confused—like a person who has fallen out of bed in the middle of the night! How will you react to this first stage of a crisis? A cardinal Truth principle is that your *reaction* to what happens to you is much more important than what happens to you!

Do you become submerged in a flood of emotion, with tears of hopelessness, helplessness, and anger? Do you look for a bottle to escape into, or a box of pills? Or can you imagine yourself holding back those surging emotions and reacting instead by affirming God's presence and power right in the teeth of the apparently crushing experience?

The Bible is, among other things, a first-aid book for emergencies, for crises. It recommends the following: " . . . *stand firm, and see the salvation of the Lord . . . .* " (Exod. 14:13) "Stand firm"—does that mean, "Don't move"? Of course not; it is referring to your inner response to the outer situation. It means, "Don't lose your sense of spiritual calm." It means remaining mentally and emotionally in that center of calmness you have developed through your meditation and prayer times.

In order to meet a crisis successfully, you must meet that first stage, that overwhelming blast-off, with a firm and unyielding realization of God's presence with you and within you, and of the invincibility of God's power. This may be difficult. I know from experience that it is much easier to say this than it is to do it. But I also know that it can be done. It calls for stretching your spiritual muscles, stretching your faith, your vision—but if you will try with all your might, you will find that those faith muscles grow strong as a result of your effort.

One very effective way to be ready for a crisis is to be armed with short, spiritually-oriented phrases that serve to patrol your field of consciousness and to fight off the intruders—those barbaric emotions of fear, panic, anger, and terror that seek to take over the citadel of your I AM.

Here are a few statements that have been valiant and successful spiritual fighters for many Truth students:

With God all things are possible.

God is my help in every need.

God is here; there is nothing to fear.

And the words *this, too, will pass,* or *things will work out,* when they are spoken from a spiritual basis, will spread oil on the stormy waters of the emotions.

When you are hit suddenly by a strange and potentially devastating experience, it may not be easy to think clearly. You may need something short, something brief, something that doesn't take a lot of words to get to the point. That is why I strongly suggest that you don't look down on some of these short, simple affirmative statements that may seem rather elementary when things are going smoothly; they can be (almost literally) life-savers when the roof seems to fall in on your life.

"Stand firm." Another way to look at this short but potent spiritual directive is this: make up your mind that this outer condition has pushed you around just as far as you are going to permit it to do. From now on you are going to take a spiritual stand, and *nothing* is going to move you. Something happens when you make up your mind to take a stand and not to retreat any further. Not only do you receive new strength, but somehow the vibration of your thought changes the entire complexion of the situation.

This is a principle that holds true spiritually and otherwise. When I was a very young lad, my family moved to a tough neighborhood. Early one evening, the local gang of kids picked on me. I cringed and cried and backed away from their threatening fists and leering faces. I felt panicky and helpless and very sorry for myself. Suddenly, though, I had had enough. I can still picture myself putting that one foot back of me and saying with my whole body, "You have pushed me this far, but that is as far as I am going to go—come what may!"

Almost immediately the entire situation changed. Just one of the fellows (we later became good friends) came toward me; the others stayed back. We wrestled and pummeled each other for a little while, but the others soon broke in; I was, as they say, "accepted."

I think you could call that a parable. It was a life-experience just like the story of the Good Samaritan or the parable of the talents; but it, too, reveals universal and timeless principles.

The appearance, the threatening condition, is given its power by you, by your fear, by your trembling response to it. Your panic seems to feed the outer condition and encourage it to grow more threatening. And the bigger and more menacing it grows, the more frightened you are. This becomes a vicious circle in which you can be trapped.

But when you "stand firm," when you say, "None of these things moves me"; when you say, "This far you have pushed me, but no further—I take my stand right here in the sure knowledge that God and I make an unbeatable team!"—then things begin to happen. All the beneficient forces of the universe rally to your aid.

Then comes the second stage of the crisis. The appearance is still there, but somehow it doesn't seem as awesome as before. You can think more clearly. You are composed enough to take time for meditation in which you do not necessarily beg for a sudden miracle. You know the miracle will come at the right time. You merely rest in the light from within. You hunger and thirst for that light to flow to you and through you as strength, as wisdom, and as understanding. If the challenge is a healing one, for instance, you acknowledge that "true light that enlightens every man" within you as a healing light, and you give thanks that it is penetrating into the very cellular structure of your body to restore, renew, revitalize, and make whole.

The third stage of a crisis is the aftermath, or the condition you are left with when the crisis is actually over. If, during the crisis, you act only from the human part of you—giving in to fear, desperation, panic, tears, self-pity—then there will be scars. You will think less of yourself, you may develop an inferiority complex, you will be more of a pushover for the next threat that comes into your life, and you will seem to attract more than your share of challenges.

But remember that although you are part human, you are also part divine. This is Jesus' teaching. How could God be your Father and you His child if there weren't something of God's overcoming nature in you?

If you have met the first two stages of the crisis with a reliance and dependence on that in you and of you that is spiritual—ever one with God—then the crisis is turned into a stepping-stone. Your faith is strengthened, your dependence on God is deepened, your self-image is reconstructed, and increasing good is attracted into your life.

The third stage—what will it be, a mess or a miracle? Try to do it yourself, all alone, reacting from the human-only part of you, and it will be a mess. But it can be a miracle! Remember that a miracle doesn't happen by chance. It is the orderly working out of spiritual law, once you take your stand. You have to do your part in establishing the conditions for the miracle to take place. This is summed up in some words spoken by Moses more than three thousand years ago: *"Fear not, stand firm, and see the salvation of the Lord, which he will work for you today . . . . "* (Exod. 14:13)

Religion is not merely a Sunday-morning tradition, a ritualistic ceremony, a cultural device for making us feel right when we are wrong. Religion, as Jesus taught and practiced it, is an ever modern, practical, effective way to meet the outer results of our own basic ignorance of who and what we are, and to meet them successfully; to grow through them, to grow in understanding, in spiritual stature, in wisdom, and in love.

Let us be still for a moment and relax into God's presence within and all around us. That Presence ever sustains and loves us. As we do this, a great peace fills our hearts and nothing can make us sad or afraid.

Be still! There is only one Presence and one Power—God. He is in us and we are in Him. This Presence in which we live, move, and have our being is ever seeking greater expression through us as increasing life, love, power, and wisdom. Let go; let God's peace calm your feverish mind. Like a lost child eagerly running to his newly found parent, let your heart run to God within you, and let it lose itself in His embrace.

The Breath of God

Putting Truth into practice is like breathing out into everyday life the activity of Spirit. The Hebrew word *spirit (ruah)* originally meant "breath." All primitive people have felt that the seat of life was in the act of breathing. The word *holy* is derived from the ancient Sanskrit word *hal,* meaning sound or whole. The Holy Spirit, then, can be understood as the universal life-essence, or God in the special aspect of activity, movement, performance, operation. The Trinity, explained in metaphysical terms, means: Father (universal Mind); Son (idea of perfect man in universal Mind); and Holy Spirit (the activity, movement, unfolding of the idea into expression).

The Holy Spirit, or the breath of God, is the whole and perfect presence of God moving through man (the Son) to guide and direct him in his individual and personal process of unfoldment. Through the Holy Spirit, Truth is put into practice in and through each of us.

189

Exercise

One purpose of these meditations is to acquaint you with a variety of ways to go within yourself in seeking your own experience of that transcendental Presence that the Bible indicates to us. There is no one correct or right way to do this; there is only the way that each individual finds effective for himself.

Because our statements deal with the Holy Spirit, and spirit means breath, let's explore the way of deep breathing. Once you are seated comfortably and relaxed, breathe in slowly, starting from the abdomen. Fill the lower abdomen with air and then continue to breathe in, filling the middle chest and then the upper chest. Now breathe out, starting with the upper chest, the middle chest, and then push every last bit of air out of the abdominal region.

This is sometimes called a "cleansing breath," for you make full use of your lungs and consciously get rid of every bid of used air. Do this a few times to set up an easy rhythm, like the ocean waves washing a sandy beach.

Now take your attention away from your breathing and rest for a bit in the light of God from within, much as you would rest on the sand and let the warm sun caress you from head to toe. Silently say: *I am resting in the light.*

The outer world is constantly trying to motivate you, to pressure you into reacting according to its demands and commands. You break its spell over you and receive your right motivation from within as you affirm: *The Holy Spirit within me is the inspiration of my soul. I am moved to right action now, and I put Truth into practice in my life.*

In doing your deep breathing exercise, you may want to speak silently the following healing statement as you hold your breath at the "top" of your inhalation, and again at that point when it is all released and before you begin the new cycle: *The Holy Spirit within me is the breath of pure life. I am healed now.*

On whom or what do you depend for your supply, your security, your wealth? In meditation, train yourself to depend on the source of all that is: *The Holy Spirit within me reveals the fullness of God's good and moves me to claim it now.*

As you continue in your meditation exercise, know for others: *The Holy Spirit—the whole Spirit of God within you—reveals His good purposes to you, and helps you to put Truth into practice in your life.*

Benediction Thought

I command my subconscious to remember that with each breath I take, I am breathing God's breath, God's life, and God's wisdom. With each breath I build a greater awareness of my inner environment of Spirit, and it is to that inner environment that I respond, on which I depend as I put Truth into practice in my life. I am grateful!

XII

If You Know It, Do It!

In this chapter, we are going to expand on one of the most important verses in the four Gospels—which, of course, are the heart of Christianity, for they contain the recorded words and teachings of Jesus. In the thirteenth chapter, the seventeenth verse, John quotes Jesus as saying: *"If you know these things, blessed are you if you do them."*

In a logjam, there is always one key log which, when found and worked on, starts the forward movement and breaks up the jam. This verse points to just that kind of mental log that may be holding up your forward progress toward more abundant, worry-free, lack-free living.

Recently a student complained to me, "I have read Truth literature for years, but I don't seem to grow spiritually. I don't have the kind of faith that will remove a molehill, much less a mountain. Things never seem to work out for me. Sometimes I think I'm no better off than someone who never heard of Truth."

Of course, this person revealed one reason for the lack of results in her first sentence, "I have read Truth literature for years." You do not get results from reading, but from practicing! Truth is to be used, not stored. *"If you know these things, blessed are you if you do them."*

This is an important point, and one that we all should give attention to—from the person who is reading this kind of teaching for the first time to those who have been familiar with Truth principles for years and years. Reading Truth books, hearing Truth talks and lessons, is inspiring. This activity appeals to the logic of the mind and gives religion a new depth of practicality. We are inspired by the illustrations of persons who have surmounted all kinds of obstacles through using Truth principles. Then we lay the book aside, or turn off the radio, or go home from the lecture, and continue in our old ways of reacting to the situations and conditions of our personal lives, keeping all our intellectual knowledge of Truth stored up in the back of our minds. But Truth is to be used, not stored!

Here is how to take Truth principles out of storage and put them into action to find a new and

exciting way of life: *discipline yourself to relate
Truth to every phase of your life*. Every phase! For
instance, do you use Truth in a supermarket? You
can, and you should. What is so strange about infinite intelligence knowing which foods are right
for you and your family and guiding you intuitively to choose them?

This might seem like a trivial thing—choosing
foods; but if you think about one of your typical
days, isn't it filled with a sequence of activities?
Each one, when lifted from the sequence, may
seem trivial; yet God can and will guide you concerning each one. Of course, you can say, "How
do I *know* that the package of food I chose was actually the right and perfect one for us?" Well,
that's just it—many times we do not "know" intellectually.

We are dealing with a power that is invisible,
silent, unable to be perceived by the five senses;
but it is a very real power! In fact, one of the first
decisions you must make when you determine to
apply the principles of the science of succesful living as taught by Jesus is to accept the premise that
there is an invisible, silent Power and Presence active in the universe and in us.

Either there is, or there isn't! If you say there is,
but you don't really believe what you are saying,
then you may as well forget about the whole idea

and go back to living with your "wits," with your intellect alone—with all the fear, uncertainty, and gnawing sense of inadequacy that the way of "intellectual living" entails.

However, if you really want to change your life, then say to yourself, "Yes, I totally accept the belief that there is a universal Power and Presence that is all-wise and all-powerful. This universal Power and Presence becomes personal to me when I provide the right conditions by totally believing in it." Then seek to acknowledge God's presence and guidance in supermarkets, at conference tables, in individual decisions in bringing up your children, in arranging a happy evening out, in helping you plan your vacation, in every facet of the sequel of events we call living.

Then you will find something happening. More things will go right in your life than will go wrong. You will find life less and less a drudgery and more a happy adventure.

This change does not come overnight, nor does it come without effort. There are times when we carefully frame an affirmation of Truth to use in dealing with a situation, and it doesn't seem to work out at all. We may feel like giving up, or we may waste our time wondering why it didn't work. Never mind asking why it didn't work out the way you thought it should or as quickly as you thought it should. *Use your Truth* on the next challenge that comes your way with undaunted confidence, for each time you use the Truth you presently understand, you grow in understanding.

If I have heard it said once, I have heard it said hundreds of times, "If only I had more time to devote to the study of Truth. But my life keeps me so busy that there isn't enough time for reading and attending classes." If you are honest with yourself, you know that this is just a clever way the personal ego has of rationalizing your procrastination about using Truth on an hour-to-hour basis. It sounds good; perhaps you *don't* have time for study. However, after living all these years, I have found that there is always time to do anything we really want to do. If you do not honestly seem to have the time, this is no bar to your growing in spiritual understanding, which is the ultimate aim of Truth books and classes.

You have some understanding of Truth or you wouldn't be making the statement that you wish you had time to study or read more. In your busy, appointment-filled, chore-filled, shopping-filled, committee-meeting-filled life, *use* the understanding you presently have. And believe me, you will make more progress than the person who reads and reads and then stores it all away and pats himself on the back for his great "knowledge" of Truth. Books and teachers give you information; *using* that information is what brings you understanding and wisdom.

You come to the point where you realize that all the Truth books are saying the same thing. Each is essentially saying: there is a universal Power and Presence which, though silent and unseen, is self-existent in the universe. You are a point of expression of this transcendent power and intelligence. By establishing the right mental conditions—that is, by believing in it, giving it your full attention and confidence—it will work through you and for you to bring about an increase of health, happiness, and prosperity in your life in spite of what seem to be impossible obstacles.

Isn't that what the Bible is saying? Isn't that what *every* Truth book is saying? So if you *know* this, you know all you really need to know about Truth. Start using the Truth you know. Start relating it to *every* phase of your life.

Recently I experienced a typical example of what may happen when we use divine guidance in making decisions. One of the contractors in our building program needed a quick decision on a part of his work that had been overlooked in the planning. It wasn't a big thing, and yet there it was. A so-called little thing can become a very important thing if we make a mistake concerning it.

While the contractor was explaining the facts of the problem, I "emptied my mind" and acknowledged the light and wisdom of God as present right there and then. As the discussion proceeded, a certain decision seemed or "felt" more right than any other. So I said, "This is it. This is what we'll do!"

To this moment I don't know for sure, intellectually, whether it was right or not. We may have to wait for the future to unfold in order to see that. But I do know that it is senseless for me to say I believe that divine guidance is available to individuals, and to spend time in meditation to make myself as receptive as possible to that guidance, and then when the time comes to call upon that guidance, to doubt whether it is right or not, and to stew and worry about it.

Did the phrase "emptied my mind" raise a question in your mind? Let me elaborate. I have found that when we have to make a decision we are not sure about, or when we have to do something we are not sure we know how to do, the best way to make ourselves receptive to transcendent wisdom and guidance is frankly to admit within ourselves that we don't know what to do! In short, if we don't know what to do, we need to admit that we don't know what to do and ask God to help us to know what to do.

That is hard on the personal ego, isn't it? This may be especially true if you are an important executive, or have earned a university degree, or if you feel a great deal of pride about your position and achievements. Our whole life is geared to help us feel that we always know what to do. That, of course, is what often creates the inner tensions and guilt feelings that we experience.

But try it. Say, *"Father-God, I don't know what to do. I empty my mind of figuring, wondering, worrying, jamming the circuits. Help me know what to do."* You will find a certain direction opening up that feels more right than any other. Follow it, and forget it. That is, don't doubt, don't worry about it. If you feel there is a logjam in your spiritual progress, rely on God, and He will provide the release and the spiritual direction you seek.

When you work with God and the spiritual forces of the universe, you will always come out on top. However, God may employ a different spiritual strategy in directing the favorable outcome of each problem, each challenge that you may meet. In meditation and prayer, you need to acknowledge the problem and admit that your finite mind does not know how to meet it. An intuitive thought will arise if you listen and wait for it. A thought that comes from infinite wisdom within you will dawn on your mind. Suddenly, while you are assessing the facts of your problem, a clear and unmistakable feeling will arise in you that if put into words will say, "Don't be afraid! Overwhelming and impossible as the outer situation may appear to be, it will be solved in a perfect way, even though I may not presently see the way."

God may employ many strategies to bring you through challenges. Many times you will be guided to do something that may bruise your ego, or that may even seem to oppose others. But if you stay close to your Source—God, your spiritual Parent—through prayer, you will know just what to do and when to do it.

Boldness is needed to really believe that God will guide and protect you at all times. You need a bold, daring, unquestioning faith that there is a transcendent Intelligence and creative Power, and that this Presence and Power is both accessible and responsive to each individual—and that means to *you*. It takes no boldness to *say* you believe in an invisible, everywhere-present God. Polls show that millions of people *say* they believe in a God. How many of those millions *act* as if there is an all-powerful God-presence that cares for them personally and is willing and able to fulfill their *every* need? If there is a God as described in the Old and New Testaments, and if millions of people say they believe in this God, then why is there so much unhappiness, so much fear, so much tension, frustration, and anger in people's lives?

I was once one of those millions. I could fool others by going to church every Sunday, but I couldn't fool myself. There just didn't seem to be any practical way in which I could relate what I heard on Sunday to my life throughout the week. So I read. I read Martin Luther, John Calvin, St. Augustine, St. Thomas Aquinas, Paul Tillich, Charles Fillmore. And finally it dawned on me that these great men and great minds were basing all their speculations and opinions on *what Jesus said and did*. The Christian religion, theoretically at least, is supposed to be a religion based squarely on the words and demonstrations of Jesus. So it dawned on me that I should try to read and understand and *follow* the teachings of Jesus.

Let's turn to a place in the New Testament where Jesus speaks about how to apply His teachings in our Monday-through-Saturday world. In the eleventh chapter, verses twenty-two through twenty-four, Mark reports the following:

And Jesus answered them, "Have faith in God. Truly, I say to you, whoever says to this mountain, 'Be taken up and cast into

*the sea,' and does not doubt in his heart,
but believes that what he says will come to
pass, it will be done for him. Therefore I tell
you, whatever you ask in prayer, believe
that you have received it, and it will be
yours."*

As I sought to implement this teaching, and as I
sought to apply it in my Monday-through-Saturday world, I could see that it would require a tremendous spiritual boldness. This is more than a
wishy-washy type of faith. If we are going to attempt to apply Jesus' teaching about how to have
prayer answered, we have to go all the way in
accepting His premise that there is an all-
powerful, miracle-working Presence and Power
that Jesus called God, the Father.

In the face of the physical world with its large
corporations, its big government, its news reports
of disasters and violence, an individual seems to
be no more than a small and ineffective ant. It
takes real boldness to say to yourself and mean it:
*There is an invisible Presence and Power that
cares personally for me. It can handle all these
huge outer forces and contrive to bring my good
to me.*

Do you have that boldness? Do you have that
spiritual courage? If you will try, then let us go on
to the next step: *mental boldness.* In Jesus' teach-

ings on how to have our prayer answered, after He said, "Have faith in God," He spoke about the importance of believing—not just believing in God, for He had covered that when He said, "Have faith in God," but believing that a *specific* need, "whatever you ask in prayer," can and will be fulfilled by God.

As an example of a specific need or request, Jesus mentioned moving a mountain into the sea. Here are the two significant points: 1) the request must be specific; and 2) we must totally believe that this specific request can and will be accomplished.

Let's begin with the specific request. Instead of just thinking about your specific need or request, write it down. A written thought is easier to handle. There it is, staring up at you from the paper. You don't have to keep going over it mentally. You may think you need and want a million things; but when you are challenged to do some clear thinking about it, clear enough so that you can write down your real needs in a straightforward and intelligible way, this may require a little thought, effort, and time.

As an example, let's say that Sally Jones finds herself bothered by the memory of how she had to take her vacation last summer at an inconvenient time. She is worrying and fretting about whether it will happen again this year. However, she has learned about the scientific application of prayer, and has decided that worrying and stewing over a problem is a waste of time. She knows that this only depletes her energies and prevents her from operating at her full potential in the present. "Don't stew about it," she tells herself, "pray about it! Get the invisible forces of the spiritual universe working on it!" So Sally gets out paper and pencil and writes down her specific need, framing it into a statement that expresses her highest conception of a perfect answer to that need. It comes out like this: *I totally accept the belief that God—whom Jesus flatly stated is aware of and loves me personally and can accomplish whatever I ask—is working through all persons and circumstances to arrange my perfect vacation. The timing will be perfect to make it the most relaxing yet exciting and fulfilling vacation of my life, and more than adequate supply will be available for it. I am grateful!*

If you feel that such a prayer is irreligious or materialistic, ask yourself these two questions:

1. Didn't Jesus say: " . . . *whatever you ask in prayer, you will receive, if you have faith"* ? (Matt. 21:22) Then, to make it clear that "whatever" means precisely that, He gave the example of moving a mountain into the sea. He didn't think

this was irreligious or materialistic; it was merely an example of what He meant when He said *"whatever you ask."*

2. Do you think God would want Sally Jones to have the wonderful vacation she described in her prayer statement? I think God would. She is His child and He loves her. Wouldn't you want the best for your children?

This is an example of how to pinpoint a problem, large or small, then frame your prayer statement in the form of a spiritually bold answer. I will always remember the ancient inscription I copied from the cornerstone of the ruins of a first-century synagogue in Capernaum during my trip to the Holy Land. It read: *Capernaum calls us to boldness of faith, because the power of God and His readiness to perform miracles are far beyond the boldest desires of our believing.*

Think big, pray big, believe big—for God's power to fulfill your prayers is equal to and greater than the very boldest of your desires! Once you have framed your prayer request in words, repeat it several times, concentrating on the words with the mental feeling that you are speaking to your subconscious mind. Then put the paper aside. Each day get it out again to look at and repeat the affirmative prayer.

The next step could be called physical boldness.

I do not mean "physical" in the sense that we associate the word with crude, overbearing actions; I mean a kind of courage to take whatever action we feel led to take concerning whatever we are praying about. Many times God can't act until *we* do. He gives us the prompting—we get an idea or a strong feeling to do a certain thing. But many times we are too timid. "What will they say? What will they think? I just don't have the nerve," we say to ourselves.

If you don't seem to have the nerve, don't blame God for not answering your prayer. Never mind what "they" may say or think. You will be successful as long as you do what you feel led to do without letting negative emotions interfere, such as "Well, I *deserve* that vacation; after all, look how unjustly I was treated last year!" When you speak or act from an emotional basis, nothing works out right. In other words, as long as you are calm and secure within, doing what you feel inwardly led to do will always turn out right in the long run for *everyone* concerned. Never mind if other people don't seem to love you for what you may say or do—*love them*. If they don't seem to be able to forgive you, *forgive them*. Keep yourself right; never mind what others are doing with their thoughts and emotions.

Remember, *first*: Prayer as Jesus taught it is

scientific. If we do certain things, provide certain conditions, we can expect definite positive results. Prayer is not founded on the whim or favor of God; it is founded on immutable spiritual principles.

Second: You must be spiritually bold by totally accepting the presence and power of that reality we call God. You must be mentally bold by thinking big, praying big, and believing big, for God can do for you only what He can do through your belief. You must also be physically bold—that is, when you have a leading to do or say a certain thing, do it, say it; remember not to act with emotion, but with calmness and kindness always. If you know the Truth, do it!

I Meet Life Courageously

In a sense, courage and love are first cousins: the word *courage* derives from the Latin word *cor*, which means heart, and the heart is thought of as the seat of love. It takes courage to love God when you seem abandoned, sick, poor, and forgotten. It takes courage to love yourself when you are well aware of your inner fears, resentments, guilt, shortcomings. It takes courage to love others when they ignore or irritate you. It takes courage to love life, when life needs positive change. Have the courage to love life, its valleys and hilltops, its triumphs and tears, and life will reward you with the kiss of immortality!

Exercise

Sit comfortably, yet attentively as you affirm: *I meet life courageously, sure that God's sustaining love is lighting the way before me, helping me to know the Truth and to do it.*

As you meditate on the statement above, catch the fire of the following synonyms for courage:

fearlessness	fortitude
resoluteness	backbone
daring	spunk
boldness	confidence

With these ideas in your mind, affirm: *I meet life courageously, knowing that God's supply is equal to every demand.* Keep your thoughts active as you dwell on these words:

determined	sticking by your guns
unshrinking	taking heart
unafraid	bulldog tenacity

Firmly know for yourself: *I meet life coura-geously, sure of God's strength, mighty to meet my every healing need.* Continue in bold thoughts as you think of the following words:

emboldened	inwardly motivated
encouraged	reassured

Concentrate your attention on these words in meditation until they seem to permeate your inner self with their power.

In this frame of mind, affirm for others: *I behold you meeting life courageously, knowing that God's love is at work and His good is unfolding, helping you to know the Truth, and to do it.*

Benediction Thought

I do not have to develop boldness and courage, for the "I AM" of me *is* spiritual boldness and courage. I simply "undevelop" the fears and doubts and procrastination tendencies I have held on to, and let the free, courageous spirit that I am shine forth. I know the Truth, and I do it in my life. I am grateful!

Printed U.S.A.

170-F-6908-20M-7-84